All You Can Do Is Pray

James Spann

Crest Publishers
124 Crest Farm Drive
Wilsonville, Alabama 35186

Copyright ♥ Pending 2021 by James Spann
124 Crest Farm Drive
Wilsonville, Alabama 35186
(205) 205-527-7785
crestpublishers@gmail.com

ISBN: 978-1-939960-56-6

Printed in the United States of America

INTRODUCTION

There is something that has kept my soul unsettled since April 27, 2011. And, unfortunately, I don't have the words to describe it. You see, I am a physical scientist, not a writer. My vocabulary is limited, much like our ability to forecast snow accurately in the Deep South.

While I have covered my share of tornadoes, severe thunderstorms, flash floods, hurricanes, heatwaves, droughts, and snowstorms in my 43-year career as a professional meteorologist, there is only one event I think about on a very regular basis. And I mean that.

At least once every few days, my mind drifts back to that warm, humid spring day that brought a generational tornado outbreak and unprecedented human suffering to my state and much of the southern U.S. I can't feel the pain directly since I didn't lose a family member that day or have my home destroyed. I didn't have to bury a child or a parent. My phone didn't ring to let me know a close relative was seriously injured, and in critical condition in some hospital.

A total of 252 Alabamians died on my watch. But I generally don't play mental gymnastics and blame myself for the loss of life. That thought would be pretty arrogant since I play only a small role in the severe weather warning process. There are many others involved and many moving parts beyond my control. But understand I am the senior broadcast meteorologist in the largest market in the state. There is a burden on me that most don't understand.

I have come to the conclusion that I have been called to tell some of the stories of April 27, 2011. Some of them were never told by journalists covering the event. I can't fault them; in a humanitarian crisis of this size, you simply don't have the time or resources. But there are instances of pain, loss, survival, perseverance, and triumph that must be shared with the world for true healing to begin. Healing in the lives of those that experienced one of those 62 tornadoes. In my life, I guess in a way there is a selfish motive for writing this book.

In my first book, "Weathering Life", I wrote mostly about my life's winding journey and career in broadcast meteorology. There was a chapter or two on April 27, 2011, but the words barely scratched the surface. I believe that if I didn't write the book you are about to read, my soul would stay unsettled until the end of my days here on Earth. Honestly, I thought "Weathering Life" would be the first and final book for me. My schedule is brutal; I work most days between 4:30 a.m. and 11:30 p.m.; there are simply not enough hours in the day to do this.

But, when you are called, you must respond. The busiest people can somehow make time for the things that are truly important to them. This book is a high priority.

There is no way I can tell every story or mention every community that suffered damage. My words cannot adequately chronicle what happened on April 27, 2011. But I have had the chance to speak with so many who describe the day in their own, powerful words. The stories here are not in any order of importance. It is simply my intention for this book to honor the lives we lost, celebrate

4

the survivors, and document a generational event for meteorologists that follow my path.

I dedicate this work to my wife Karen; we have now been married just about 40 years as the book is released. She has been the unwavering one on my side through it all, including April 27, 2011. It isn't easy being married to a broadcast meteorologist due to the bad hours, the intense pressure, blown snow forecasts, social media trolls, and the general craziness of it all. It is also dedicated to our two sons, J.P. and Ryan. Words can't describe the gratitude for my family's support through this journey. I love them very much.

CHAPTER 1: THE SEASON

"To every thing there is a season, and a time to every purpose under the heaven." Ecclesiastes 3:1

There are two well-defined areas where tornado activity tends to occur at a maximum across the United States. The Great Plains, and the Deep South. I chuckle when I see researchers and practitioners arguing about who has the "biggest, baddest" tornadoes. Oklahoma City, or Birmingham? Wichita or Jackson? To me, that dialogue isn't very productive... It is like two dogs fussing about which one hosts the highest flea population. Let's just say that both regions feature some very productive tornado seasons.

My focus is the southern U.S. I am the chief meteorologist for the ABC TV affiliate in Birmingham and can testify to the magnitude and power of the severe weather events here. Since 1978, I have been forecasting and covering Alabama's weather, including countless tornado days.

Around here for a long time I would tell people we have two distinct severe weather seasons... one in late fall and early winter, and another one in the spring. But I can honestly say I have changed my tune in recent years. My message now is that we have one primary tornado season: November through May. Yes, we can have tornadoes from June through October, but those are usually associated with landfalling hurricanes or tropical storms and are entirely different creatures.

I just don't believe there is enough of a drop in tornado activity in January and February to not consider it part of a continuous severe weather season. During my teenage years, and the time when I was falling in love with the science of meteorology, events like the Pell City, Alabama tornado of January 10, 1975, and the Tuscaloosa, Alabama tornado of February 23, 1975, taught me well about the convective potential of those two months.

The Pell City tornado was rated F3 and was one of at least 13 tornadoes that touched down across Alabama on January 10, 1975. Five of the tornadoes were rated as F2 or higher. One person was killed, and over sixty were injured.

Below is the storm summary of the damaged area written by Bob Ferry, the Meteorologist-In-Charge at the time of the National Weather Service in Birmingham:

"Friday afternoon January 10, 1975, a tornado moved northeastward across the center of downtown Pell City, Alabama, and stopped at the First National Bank Clock at 4:11 p.m. Many buildings, mostly homes, were heavily damaged by large trees (some five to six feet in diameter near the trunk) uprooted and falling across them. Seven mobile homes were completely destroyed in a small trailer park (Smith's) which is about one mile northeast of Pell City. The Red Cross reported that 33 people were taken to the hospital for treatment where only three were admitted - those, not too serious. There were no injuries in the trailer park because residents had taken shelter in a nearby brick building. None of the trailers had tie-downs."

One month later, the Tuscaloosa tornado (rated F4) of February 23, 1975, passed within one mile of me on that Sunday afternoon. A very close rendezvous with a killer tornado; I can still hear the roar. I was an 18-year-old college student working at WTBC radio, the BIG 1230, in Tuscaloosa, playing the hits. I received a tornado warning via a Civil Defense alert radio we had in the studio (this was before NOAA Weather Radio was operational), and passed the warning along to our audience about ten minutes before it rolled through the city and power was lost at the station.

WTBC was on 15th Street, less than one mile west of the tornado path that cut through the southern and eastern parts of Tuscaloosa. There was particularly heavy damage near I-59 and McFarland Blvd. Most of the upper floor of the Scottish Inn was torn away, killing one housekeeper named Thelma Hill.

Of the seven months I consider tornado season, the highest occurrence comes in April. Alabama experienced 41 tornadoes in the month during the year 2020 bringing the April total since 1950 to 550. March is a distant second with 328 tornadoes during the same period.

April is the month when the mid-latitude westerly winds aloft are in a perfect position to bring dynamic troughs with very strong wind fields in the upper atmosphere through the southern U.S... interacting with warm, moist, buoyant air that has lifted northward from the Gulf of Mexico. Throw in a few small-scale boundaries, and the stage is set for violent weather.

For those of us in operational meteorology, April is a month when you never plan a vacation. Don't even think about it; you don't want to be in the Bahamas when strong/violent tornadoes are bearing down on Alabama. I do school science weather programs daily, sometimes two a day in the spring. But every teacher that books a program with me knows there is danger of a cancellation due to severe weather potential in April.

And, we all know that severe weather events don't necessarily come at convenient times. The big storms can roll in during the pre-dawn hours or on weekends. You have to be ready for everything at any hour of the day or night this time of the year. And, for me personally, that is no problem. I believe I was born to do this, and it is my honor to work some odd, sleepless hours in an effort to mitigate the loss of life.

My first vacation week every year comes in June when we have calmer days.

CHAPTER 2: THE FORGOTTEN TORNADO OUTBREAK

I am not a big fan of seasonal outlooks. Nothing wrong with them, I guess, and there are certainly many in our science who are qualified to issue them. Good examples are the hurricane outlooks issued in the spring that look ahead to the tropical season in the Atlantic basin. The accuracy of them is less than stellar, and I wonder how those products are used by the public and emergency managers. All you need is one big hurricane striking a major coastal city... we have to be ready every hurricane season whether you have fifteen hurricanes or just one.

To my knowledge, there are no "official" tornado season outlooks, but many do offer their opinion. Most tend to look at the ENSO (El Niño Southern Oscillation) phase, but the correlation is not very precise. The record-setting tornado outbreaks during April 2011 took place within a global climate context of lingering La Niña conditions (cold phase of the Southern Oscillation). But, according to NOAA's Physical Sciences Laboratory, their analysis covering 1950-2003 found that neither the frequency of tornado days nor of violent tornado days (days with five or more F2+ tornadoes) is affected systematically by the ENSO phase for the U.S. as a whole.

A separate investigation that used data for a shorter period of 1950-1992, but covering all seasons, argued that La Niña events did increase tornadic activity in the Ohio River Valley and the Deep South during spring, and that La Niña facilitates large tornadic outbreaks and is associated with more destructive storms.

The bottom line is that more research is required to determine the extent to which La Niña itself is a meaningful and useful early warning indicator for U.S. severe weather.

As a result, going into the spring of 2011, like always we were ready for anything that would happen. But I possessed no knowledge of the historic events to come as April began.

On April 11, a short-lived EF-1 tornado moved through parts of Vestavia Hills, in the southern part of the Birmingham metro area. It was down for about a third of a mile and knocked down over 100 trees; thankfully there were no injuries. There was also considerable straight-line wind damage across parts of Jefferson and Shelby counties. Based on what we know now, it seems like this event was a harbinger -- an anticipatory sign of what was to come.

Just four days later, on April 15, Alabama would experience a red-letter severe weather day -- one for the record books. This was the middle day of a three-day outbreak that struck from across the Plains to the East Coast of the U.S. during April 14-16. During this event, a total of 178 tornadoes touched down in Oklahoma, Texas, Arkansas, Kansas, Mississippi, Alabama, Georgia, Kentucky, Missouri, Illinois, South Carolina, North Carolina, Virginia, Maryland, and Pennsylvania. A total of 38 people lost their lives, and another 588 people were injured.

On that Friday, April 15, a total of 45 tornadoes touched down across Alabama, most of them concentrated over the southwest counties of the state. One EF-3 developed west of Moundville, near the point where Hale, Greene, and Tuscaloosa counties come together along the Black Warrior River. It would go on into the southern and eastern parts of the city of Tuscaloosa. Along this path, damage consisted of snapped or uprooted trees and structural damage to homes and businesses. The tornado lifted near Mayfair Drive, south of Veterans Memorial Parkway. The tornado damage path was 18.37 miles long and was 500 yards wide at its widest point. Thankfully, a timely warning was issued, people were paying attention, and there were no deaths or serious injuries.

However, our state did experience loss of life that day; another EF-3 struck the Boones Chapel community in far northern Autauga County. This twister was the third one to affect the same general area that day. Three people were killed and four were seriously injured as the tornado destroyed their manufactured home. In all, at least 50 homes and one business were either destroyed or significantly damaged by this one.

Again, I believe the weather events of April 15, 2011, were a harbinger. The atmosphere was talking to us. Telling a story. Letting us know what it was capable of producing with the juxtaposition of atmospheric Rossby waves and moist, unstable air from the Gulf of Mexico.

The April 15, 2011 event is called the "forgotten outbreak". Yes, those directly impacted by a tornado that day remember, but for most Alabamians it simply doesn't register because of what would happen 12 days later.

CHAPTER 3: THE SETUP

Many research papers have been authored over the past decade concerning the atmospheric setup in April 2011. One of them was put together by three friends and mentors that I respect greatly…. Charles A. Doswell III, Harold Brooks, and Greg Carbin. If you are seriously interested in severe local convective storms, search out papers from these guys. Their work is brilliant. They write:

"The large-scale pattern during the last two weeks of April was dominated by a broad upper-level trough on the average across the middle of the country. This trough was anomalously deep for this time of year across the north-central USA and much of western Canada; meanwhile, upper-level ridging was anomalously strong along the east coast and over the Atlantic.

It should be noted that this average pattern resulted in several traveling extratropical cyclones (ETCs) during the period, encouraging their development in the southern plains of the USA and intensification as they moved northeastward. This pattern favored the northward transport of moisture at low levels and the eastward transport of high lapse rates above that moisture, so the lapse rates and moisture during this period were also highly anomalous and further supported the potential for widespread severe thunderstorms. The ETCs tied to the large-scale trough had strong fronts and drylines to provide the necessary lift of the moist, unstable air. The gradient between the pronounced upper-level height anomalies provides a particularly strong jet stream and associated vertical wind shear that is the other necessary ingredient for supercells and tornadoes."

They are basically saying all of the players were on the field for major severe weather problems.

*Strong rising atmospheric motion east of the deep, mean upper trough over the Central U.S.

*Vigorous wind fields, both at the surface and aloft

*Diffluence aloft, and convergence below

*A deep surface low migrating northeast, providing strong veering of the wind with altitude

*Steep lapse rates; temperatures dropped quickly with height

*Rich low-level moisture

*Highly unstable air that is buoyant

*A layer of dry air in the mid-levels

*A low lifting condensation level (LCL), a measure that has shown some skill in differentiating tornadic and non-tornadic supercell environments

*Small-scale boundaries that helped to provide "backed" surface winds (turning of a south or southwest surface wind with time to a more east or southeasterly direction)

*Climatology. It is all coming together in April, the month when severe weather mischief is expected. The big one.

It is my job to take all of these parameters, analyze them, and communicate the potential danger in a sensible, calm, easy-to-understand way to the public across all platforms, including TV, commercial radio, digital (blogs, etc.), and social (Facebook, Twitter, etc.).

NWP (numerical weather prediction) is one of our major tools in weather forecasting... better known as good ole computer models. Sure, they can lead you down the wrong path sometimes, but to me they represent a true accomplishment in physical science. The accuracy of these models is remarkable considering the chaotic nature of the Earth's atmosphere and the lack of constant, real-time upper-air data (that input is critical to the success of model runs).

Both major global models meteorologists use, the American (GFS, run by NOAA) and the one from the European Center for Medium-Range Weather Forecasts (ECMWF), advertised the potent setup five to seven days in advance. Of course, those models don't have the grid resolution (13 to 16 km in 2011) to handle small-scale boundaries and features that are critical in severe thunderstorm formation far in advance, but they are very accurate on the synoptic scale.

On Wednesday, April 20, 2011, I wrote this in the afternoon discussion on our blog, alabamawx.com:

"Another dynamic spring storm system will develop over the nation's midsection, setting the stage for another

round of severe weather, which should begin Monday over the Great Plains, then spreading east. Still looks like the main threat for Alabama will come late Tuesday, Tuesday night, and perhaps into Wednesday morning. Still too early to determine the exact timing or the greatest threats. Stay tuned."

We were able to identify the severe weather potential one week in advance, although the timing was off by 12-18 hours. Not bad that far out.

I was hitting it much harder by Friday, April 22:

"Still looks like a significant severe weather event coming up for the southern U.S. The problems begin early in the week to the west; showers and storms could arrive in Alabama as early as Tuesday, but the main event seems to be Wednesday, and the 12Z GFS hints that all modes of severe weather will be possible; cellular supercell storms Wednesday afternoon, followed by a squall line with potential for damaging winds Wednesday night. And, heavy rain will be an issue as well. We will keep an eye on this over the weekend and have a detailed look by Monday."

This was just right before the Easter weekend, and I wanted people to know of the potential situation. We walk a fine line between letting people know of potentially dangerous weather and weather hyperbole. In 2011, the social media fearmongers weren't too much of a problem. These are people who don't know much about how the atmosphere works, and the limitations of our science figured out the key to getting likes, follows, and shares is to throw out scary forecasts of tornadoes, hurricanes, and

18

winter storms weeks in advance. The more the hype, the more followers you get. And, oddly enough, people don't seem to mind if they are wrong 90 percent of the time. It is a huge problem we fight today.

But on April 22, 2011, we were within five days of the event, and there is very adequate skill in an event forecast that far out. The possibility had to be mentioned. It was the responsible thing to do.

Let's jump ahead to Monday, April 25, 2011. These were my words concerning the weather over the next 72 hours:

"We will be dealing with all modes of severe weather through Wednesday night. Tomorrow, the main threat will be from strong straight winds and hail, but a tornado can't be ruled out. I expect a weakening line of storms to move into Northwest Alabama tomorrow morning, but we all know those can pack a punch long beyond when you expect them to die out. Then, new storms will likely form tomorrow afternoon into tomorrow night in the unstable air.

The primary threat of tornadoes will come on Wednesday afternoon when supercells will begin to form across North and Central Alabama as the cap breaks. Forecast wind profiles and instability values suggest a few strong, long-track tornadoes will be possible across the northern half of Alabama Wednesday afternoon into the evening hours."

This is when we really started to hit it hard across the weather enterprise. We clearly mentioned the potential for violent, long-track tornadoes in our messaging for April 27, hoping people would listen and prepare.

I pushed this hard across all of my platforms -- on ABC 33/40, my commercial radio affiliates, the blog (alabamawx.com), and social media (mainly Facebook and Twitter). The iPhone was four years old in 2011, and many still didn't have a smartphone. Social media was new. Old school television and radio were still the main ways of getting the word out at the time.

And, understand it wasn't just me; other local broadcast meteorologists, the National Weather Service, and emergency managers did a very good job of spreading the word. We just prayed that people heard the message and responded by being prepared.

Then, on Tuesday, April 26, these were some of my words on the blog:

DANGEROUS SEVERE WEATHER THREAT TOMORROW: Watch the video and you will see all of the synoptic elements for a major outbreak are in place. A deep (sub-1000 mb) low west of Memphis, steep lapse rates, strong veering of the wind with altitude in respect to projected storm motion, strong wind fields at the surface and aloft, dry air in the mid-levels, and a very deep, long-wave upper trough that is somewhat negatively tilted enhancing diffluence aloft over Alabama.

Projected soundings show the classic "loaded gun" look, meaning that a cap should keep storms at bay through the morning hours, but when that cap breaks early in the afternoon, storms will quickly become severe with all modes of severe weather possible. This means potential for large hail, damaging winds, and a few violent, long-track tornadoes. This is a dangerous weather setup.

REMEMBER: With the potential for some severe weather today, and a red-letter kind of severe weather day possible tomorrow, be sure you are in a position to hear severe weather warnings (never rely on a siren!), and have a good plan of action when warnings are issued. No need to panic; even large tornadoes are small compared to a large county. But we must be prepared.

SCHOOLS: For school systems that do decide to dismiss early tomorrow, please consider giving students that live in mobile homes the option of staying in school buildings. In many rural parts of the state those school buildings are absolutely the safest place.

Turned out the morning round of storms the following day would be much more robust than I expected, but the message was clear. If you hear me call an event a "red-letter" kind of day, you better be ready for some serious, life-threatening weather. I don't use those words often.

CHAPTER 4: IT BEGINS

Even on routine days, I work long hours. I begin with an alarm at 4:52 a.m., and usually get home around midnight. I haven't slept much since 1973, the year I first took a job at WTBC radio in Tuscaloosa when I was in high school. I am not sure what almost 50 years of sleep deprivation will do to a person, but I guess I will find out in the fourth quarter of my life, which I am entering now.

I got home on April 26, 2011, around the usual time, close to midnight. As you might expect, I really had a hard time getting to sleep. For a meteorologist on the eve of any big event, it is very challenging, if not impossible, to turn off your mind for needed rest.

All of the severe weather parameters were in place for a major outbreak, but I still didn't know exactly how it all would unfold. Could it be a "high risk" bust? If so, would people forgive me for crying wolf? Could it potentially be a historic weather day? Would people lose their lives? I knew there was strong possibility that for a few Alabamians, their next day on Earth would be the next day. Who are they and where do they live? I sure hoped I did enough to get people ready.

I finally drifted off to sleep about 1:00 a.m. as I recall.

But, instead of getting up at the usual 4:52, an alarm sounded around 4:00 a.m. when a tornado warning was issued for Pickens County in the far western part of Alabama. There was no time to think and analyze what was going on, I just had to react. My colleague, Jason Simpson, was at the station by himself, since we had planned for full staffing during the afternoon and nighttime hours. Jason was and still is fully capable of handling tornado warnings on his own but it is pretty tough for a TV meteorologist with no help.

I took, most likely, the quickest shower in my life, and drove at a frantic pace to the ABC 33/40 Studio in Riverchase. The drive from my home is usually about 25 minutes, but I made it in 15 minutes that morning. I figured any officers that might pull me over would have compassion and understand the situation, but as I recall I barely saw any other cars on the road at that insane hour of the morning.

As I walked into the station, Jason was, as always, doing an exemplary job on the air handling the pre-dawn storms. He was in control, calm, knowledgeable, and told people exactly what they needed to know in a clear, concise way. I joined him, and we stayed on the air until 9:00 a.m. when all warnings for our DMA (Designated Market Area) had expired.

I first met Jason when he was a student at Holly Pond High School. It was clear that he had a genuine interest in weather, and would do very well if he chose to pursue a career in meteorology. I am sure glad he followed his dream; I would not have wanted to be with anyone else that day.

Jason interned with me while he was a meteorology student at Mississippi State, and would go on to work at stations in Mississippi and Missouri before he joined ABC 33/40. I am thankful for our long years of friendship, but this was the day that will always bind us together.

The morning round of storms was more intense and had much more impact than I expected the night before. The QLCS (Quasi Linear Convective System) produced widespread wind damage as it moved across the state. Oftentimes, a QLCS will create small spin-ups, or rotational areas, on the front edge of the line. These spin-ups typically result in a weak EF-0 or EF-1 tornado. But on the morning of April 27, 2011, the spin-ups were much more robust; there were three tornadoes rated EF-3, and five rated EF-2.

The more notable tornadoes that morning included...

*An EF-3 that moved through Cordova, in Walker County, injuring 20 people. What people didn't know at the time was that another, stronger tornado would hit the same community later in the day bringing loss of life.

*An EF-3 at Coaling, east of Tuscaloosa, close to the Mercedes Plant in Vance.

*An EF-2 at Cahaba Heights, in the southern part of the Birmingham metro area. At least 20 were injured in this highly populated area. We were very fortunate that there was no loss of life.

Some of the most intense straight-line damage during the morning hours was found in St. Clair County at Moody, Pell City, and Riverside. Two of the deaths came in those areas when trees fell on mobile homes.

The morning storms left about a quarter of a million people with no power in Alabama. We knew this could be a big issue going forward; the "big show" was to come later in the day, and this lack of power would seriously impair the warning process. People would not be able to watch long form coverage on TV, NOAA Weather Radio receivers would be out of service for those without a battery backup, and the inability for people would be unable to charge their phones.

And, right after we got off the air with the first round of long form coverage, ABC 33/40 engineers flooded the weather office to tell us we had some major infrastructure damage. Some SKYCAMs were down. Microwave paths out. It really didn't sound good. We were about to begin a generational severe weather event, and we were severely crippled.

I finally had to change the conversation; understanding what wasn't working was fine, but I had to know what WAS working. And, we had to prioritize the repair process. There was much to do and very little time.

To their credit, Ron Thomas and his engineering team did a remarkable job of getting many of the SKYCAMs back online during the midday lull. The one in Cullman would later show the world the disaster unfolding across the American South in just a few hours.

Funny thing, I started seeing some buzz on social media about how we were wrong. The storms had come early in the day instead of during the afternoon and nighttime hours, and now the sun was out. It was a beautiful day; no need for any more concern. Haters and trolls were out in full force.

Of course, the sunshine meant warmer surface temperatures, which in turn is part of the destabilization process needed for more severe weather. We did our best to remind people that the worst was yet to come; they needed to be ready, and they needed to have a good way of hearing watches and warnings. This was an extremely dangerous situation, and with so many power outages people needed to get creative in ways of hearing tornado warnings.

I honestly don't recall if I had any lunch. Probably not; we were just too busy trying to sort out the equipment issues and get ready for the afternoon. It was all a blur. And, there was certainly no rest for the weary.

CHAPTER 5: CULLMAN

As expected, showers and thunderstorms developed quickly by early afternoon in the powder keg environment over Alabama. A "PDS" (Particularly Dangerous Situation) tornado watch was issued by the Storm Prediction Center at 1:45p.m. CT, which would be in effect until 10:00p.m. CT. This covered most of Alabama and some of the adjacent states. It was a timely watch that clearly stated the potential for strong/violent, long-track tornadoes.

```
URGENT – IMMEDIATE BROADCAST REQUESTED
TORNADO WATCH NUMBER 235
NWS STORM PREDICTION CENTER NORMAN OK
145 PM CDT WED APR 27 2011

THE NWS STORM PREDICTION CENTER HAS ISSUED A
TORNADO WATCH FOR PORTIONS OF

MUCH OF ALABAMA
NORTHWEST GEORGIA
SOUTHEAST MISSISSIPPI
SOUTHERN MIDDLE TENNESSEE

EFFECTIVE THIS WEDNESDAY AFTERNOON AND EVENING FROM 145 PM UNTIL
1000 PM CDT.

...THIS IS A PARTICULARLY DANGEROUS SITUATION...

DESTRUCTIVE TORNADOES...LARGE HAIL TO 4 INCHES IN DIAMETER...
THUNDERSTORM WIND GUSTS TO 80 MPH...AND DANGEROUS LIGHTNING ARE
POSSIBLE IN THESE AREAS.

THE TORNADO WATCH AREA IS APPROXIMATELY ALONG AND 80 STATUTE
MILES EAST AND WEST OF A LINE FROM 45 MILES NORTHEAST OF
HUNTSVILLE ALABAMA TO 60 MILES WEST SOUTHWEST OF EVERGREEN
ALABAMA. FOR A COMPLETE DEPICTION OF THE WATCH SEE THE
ASSOCIATED WATCH OUTLINE UPDATE (WOUS64 KWNS WOU5).

REMEMBER...A TORNADO WATCH MEANS CONDITIONS ARE FAVORABLE FOR
TORNADOES AND SEVERE THUNDERSTORMS IN AND CLOSE TO THE WATCH
AREA. PERSONS IN THESE AREAS SHOULD BE ON THE LOOKOUT FOR
THREATENING WEATHER CONDITIONS AND LISTEN FOR LATER STATEMENTS
AND POSSIBLE WARNINGS.

OTHER WATCH INFORMATION...CONTINUE...WW 230...WW 231...WW
232...WW 233...WW 234...

DISCUSSION...A CLASSIC TORNADO OUTBREAK SITUATION IS DEVELOPING
ACROSS MUCH OF AL AS DISCRETE TORNADIC SUPERCELLS FORM OVER MS AND
TRACK ACROSS THE WATCH AREA. STRONG LOW LEVEL AND DEEP LAYER
VERTICAL SHEAR...COMBINED WITH A MOIST AND MODERATELY UNSTABLE AIR
MASS...WILL POSE A DANGEROUS RISK OF STRONG/VIOLENT AND POTENTIALLY
LONG-TRACK TORNADOES.
```

While SPC issues the severe weather watches from their facility in Norman, Oklahoma, local National Weather Service offices issue the actual warnings. In Alabama, most of the warnings on April 27, 2011, were issued by NWS offices in Birmingham and Huntsville. The men and women who work there don't get as much visibility as we do in the television industry, but their work was crucial that day. They were some of the "unsung heroes".

When that tornado watch was issued, I went on the air with absolutely no intention of going back to regular programming. Birmingham is a very aggressive severe weather market, and we are "wall to wall" anytime a single county in the market is under a tornado warning.

You need to go back to 1996 for the start of our policy; I left WBRC that year to join the new station in town, ABC 33/40, during an affiliation swap. The Allbritton family put the station on the air, and they gave me the total green light for long form, wall to wall tornado coverage. I never had that liberty at the stations where I previously worked, yet, here I was free to do anything and everything to ensure the people of this state knew that life-threatening weather was approaching. I am thankful to Robert Allbritton to this day for changing the way severe weather is handled in the Birmingham market.

There were no tornado warnings in effect when that watch was issued at 1:45, but I knew they would be coming very shortly. I decided to terminate the regular programming and go to full weather coverage in order to alert people of the impending severe weather. No need to go back to "General Hospital"; you can watch that another day. I'm sure some nitwits somewhere sent me nasty notes about missing "their story", but anyone griping about that on this day is beyond hope.

Sure enough, the first tornado warning of the afternoon was issued at 2:09p.m. CT for parts of Walker and Winston counties in North Alabama. A storm north of Jasper was showing strong signs of producing a tornado, and moving northeast. Then, fifteen minutes later, a warning was also issued for Cullman County as the tornadic storm was over Smith Lake.

As this supercell approached the city of Cullman, we scanned the western horizon with our Cullman SKYCAM, located at the water treatment facility just east of downtown Cullman on U.S. 278. The camera there is on a high perch and gives a great view of the weather in all directions. And, remember, this is one of the cameras that went down during the morning round of storms.

Jason and I didn't expect to see much with the storm still well to the southwest of the city and knowing that tornadoes in Alabama are rain-wrapped due to the HP (Heavy Precipitation) type supercells we see here. But, to our surprise, we actually had a good shot into the right rear flank of the storm, and for sure, a wall cloud was visible. We didn't know for certain if a tornado was down, but there was certainly a high probability based on the radar signature and the environmental conditions.

Within a few minutes, the tornado was visible on the SKYCAM, and we called a "tornado emergency" for the city of Cullman. Our warning was an urgent call for everyone in the path of the storm to take action IMMEDIATELY. Small room, lowest floor, near the center, away from windows. No vehicles, no mobile homes. Put on a helmet if you can. Sure, most people in Alabama know this, but we have to remember we have many people who are new to our state and have not experienced anything like this before.

The population of Cullman in 2010 was 14,775, and this tornado was moving right toward the heart of the city. Not a good situation.

We know now this was one of eight EF-4 tornadoes that would touch down that day in Alabama. This violent storm moved right into downtown Cullman, as expected, and the world watched it live through that SKYCAM. The Weather Channel took our coverage live, along with some other national cable news networks.

We watched the tornado take down a free-standing communications tower adjacent to First Baptist Church, along U.S. 31 in the middle of town. Then, we watched parts of the Cullman County Courthouse being lofted right before the power failed at the SKYCAM site.

The Cullman EF-4 tornado, live on ABC 33/40 April 27, 2011. This SKYCAM is atop the water treatment plant, just east of downtown Cullman on U.S. 278.

My heart was sinking as I watched that live SKYCAM video while we were on the air knowing at least 15,000 people were in the direct path of the storm. No doubt there could be catastrophic damage, but beyond that, the potential for loss of life was very high.

One thing you need to understand is that I am a native Alabamian. I was born here and I have worked most of my 43-year career here. I will die here and will be buried here. These are my people. I have spent all these years with daily road trips across the state, doing weather programs in schools, and for homeschool groups. I would never be able to count the number of senior adult lunches I have attended and delivered a rambling talk about southern life and weather. Too many Rotary Club meetings and safety meetings for large businesses to count.

I consider all Alabamians as part of my family. Like any family, we have fights and disagreements along the way, but I love the people of this state. And for some reason, I believe I was born to be standing in front of a big green wall on April 27, 2011, to take care of them. This was a battle that day to protect precious human life. I take the responsibility personally and seriously.

Our news folks called the Cullman Regional Medical Center shortly after the tornado had moved through. To our surprise, everyone was fine. Sure, they had some there with cuts and bruises, but there were no critical injuries and no loss of life. I thought to myself, maybe, just maybe, we could get through the "big show" that afternoon with no fatalities.

The warning system in this case worked very well. People in Cullman County knew how to get the warning, even with so many power outages. When they turned to us, they saw the tornado live on the SKYCAM, and they knew what to do. They got into safe places, and despite widespread structural damage, everyone survived. We can rebuild a business, school, or church... we just have to be sure people can survive.

Quite frankly, working the Cullman tornado was easy for us. At the time, this was the only tornadic thunderstorm in the entire state. We didn't have to bounce back and forth between storms, we could focus on that one supercell all the way with no interruption.

As the tornado moved out of Cullman County, a new tornado warning was issued at 2:59p.m. CT for another storm in Northeast Mississippi; the warning in Alabama was for parts of Lamar and Marion counties. Then, at 3:15p.m. CT, a tornado warning was issued for parts of Pickens and Tuscaloosa counties in West Alabama. With one glance at the radar, you knew this was going to be one of the most difficult days in Alabama weather history.

CHAPTER 6: BULLETS FROM HELL

We all know now exactly what happened on April 27, 2011. You can see maps that show all of the tornadoes, their tracks, and the ratings on the Enhanced Fujita (EF) scale. A total of 62 tornadoes in Alabama. But, remember during the event itself we didn't know exactly what each thunderstorm was producing. Every supercell had to be treated seriously. Some produced violent tornadoes, others produced weaker tornadoes or strong straight-line winds. The one thing we did know is that all of them were extremely dangerous, and people had to be sheltered for every storm that evening. And, I mean EVERY storm.

The severe storm that developed over Marion County, and prompted the tornado warning for parts of Lamar and Marion counties at 2:59p.m. CT, would wind up producing what was most likely the most ferocious tornado of the day in Alabama.

BULLETIN – EAS ACTIVATION REQUESTED
TORNADO WARNING
NATIONAL WEATHER SERVICE BIRMINGHAM AL
259 PM CDT WED APR 27 2011

THE NATIONAL WEATHER SERVICE IN BIRMINGHAM HAS ISSUED A

* TORNADO WARNING FOR...
NORTH CENTRAL LAMAR COUNTY IN WEST CENTRAL ALABAMA...
NORTHERN MARION COUNTY IN NORTHWEST ALABAMA...

* UNTIL 345 PM CDT

* AT 256 PM CDT...THE NATIONAL WEATHER SERVICE INDICATED A SEVERE
THUNDERSTORM CAPABLE OF PRODUCING A TORNADO. THIS DANGEROUS STORM
WAS LOCATED NEAR DETROIT...OR 12 MILES NORTHWEST OF SULLIGENT...AND
MOVING NORTHEAST AT 55 MPH.

* LOCATIONS IMPACTED INCLUDE...
HAMILTON...WESTON...HACKLEBURG...BYRD...RANKIN FITE AIRPORT...
SHOTSVILLE...TESSNER AND BEAR CREEK.

THIS INCLUDES...
US 78 EXIT NUMBERS 3 THROUGH 14...

PRECAUTIONARY/PREPAREDNESS ACTIONS...

MOTORISTS SHOULD NOT TAKE SHELTER UNDER HIGHWAY OVERPASSES. AS A LAST
RESORT...EITHER PARK YOUR VEHICLE AND STAY PUT...OR ABANDON YOUR
VEHICLE AND LIE DOWN IN A LOW LYING AREA.

A violent, rare, EF-5 tornado dropped out of this
thunderstorm, passing just north of Hamilton, then
moving toward the community of Hackleburg. The
tornado tracked parallel to US Highway 43 toward
Hackleburg and strengthened with winds up to 210 mph,
as its path widened to 0.75 mile (1320 yds). Several
subdivisions and businesses, Hackleburg High School,
Middle School, and Elementary School, and the Wrangler

Plant were destroyed. Vehicles were tossed up to 200 yards. One well-built home with four brick sides was completely leveled and the debris from the home was tossed over 40 yards to the north. My words are not sufficient to describe the disaster.

From Hackleburg, the storm moved through Phil Campbell, and on into Lawrence, Morgan, Limestone, and Madison counties in the Tennessee Valley of North Alabama.

There is no doubt in my mind this was the most violent tornado of the day in Alabama, although two other EF-5s did touch down. This single tornado was responsible for the deaths of 72 Alabamians, making it the deadliest single tornado ever to strike the state of Alabama. In addition to being the deadliest, this tornado also had the longest track of any tornado in the outbreak, with its path extending 132.1 miles across North Alabama and into Tennessee.

By 4:00p.m. CT, the radar images were nothing less than terrifying. Remember, we were in "wall to wall" coverage, and being the guy on the green wall didn't allow much time to reflect on the historic nature of what was happening. I was simply too busy looking at messages across the various NWS (National Weather Service) online chat sessions, social media pictures and video from viewers, live streams from our Skywatchers in the field, and trying to stay coherent on the air with an easy to understand and calm presentation. But my mind did drift back very briefly to the "Superoutbreak" of April 3, 1974, when I was a high school senior. I worked the event that night in the Emergency Operations Center of

Tuscaloosa County Civil Defense, and would later be sent northward to set up my amateur radio gear in some of the hardest hit places to establish links to relief agencies.

My first assignment was in Jasper at the People's Hospital. I was sent to the emergency room, where I set up the gear and got them in touch with the needed agencies in Birmingham. During my time there I saw the serious side of weather. Words can't describe the graphic nature of the wounds people had as they were rushed into the small ER. Some were dead on arrival, others in very critical condition. For some reason, I think I had to experience that night in 1974 as part of the preparation for my long weather career. I had to do everything in my power to keep people from being hurt like that or losing their lives on April 27, 2011. I was dealing with bullets from hell.

Around 4:15p.m. CT, the focus was on two supercell storms. One was moving just south of the community of Berry, near the Fayette/Tuscaloosa county line. Another was crossing the Tombigbee River, south of Gainesville in West Alabama. Both of these had the "look" on radar - a classic hook echo, debris ball, and velocity couplet.

This was before we had dual-polarization Doppler Radar, meaning no correlation coefficient products and the ability to detect lofted debris. But in this case we didn't have to have it. We knew these two storms were most likely producing an upper end violent tornado.

In terms of communication, I had a real dilemma later in the hour. The northern supercell was in Walker County, about to cross Interstate 22, and Brian Peters and Tim Coleman had a visual on the storm; it was producing a large, wedge tornado as feared. I didn't have live video from them, but I had them on the phone.

At the exact same time, John Oldshue and Ben Greer had a live video stream of the southern supercell near the Greene/Tuscaloosa county line. Like the Walker County storm, a violent tornado was down. Understand, getting a live stream of this massive tornado in such a rural area was quite the feat in 2011. But these guys had connectivity and were in the right place at the right time.

I had a split second to make a decision. How do I communicate the urgency of both storms? I went with John's live video stream southwest of Tuscaloosa, while at the same time I brought in Brian and Tim on the phone to describe the storm approaching Cordova. History will judge that decision; I hope it didn't create confusion. Video of a storm in one place, audio describing a separate storm somewhere else. It was the best I could do at the time.

I called both situations a "tornado emergency" on the air, and with the most urgency possible I told people in the path of the storms to get into a safe place IMMEDIATELY.

Yet, within one hour of this warning, 13 people would lose their lives in Cordova; over 50 died in Tuscaloosa. Was the messaging not clear? Did I confuse people? I honestly don't know the answer, but on the other hand, I do know that lives were saved in both places because of the work done by Oldshue, Greer, Peters, and Coleman.

41

I have the easiest job on the team. I am in a dry, safe studio with everything I need at my fingertips. Working a tornado outbreak in the field is beyond challenging; it is dangerous. I will never take their work for granted.

Cordova was hit by the EF-4 twister shortly before 5:00p.m. CT; from there it would go on through other parts of Walker County around Sipsey and Empire, and then crossing the southern tip of Cullman County, it then moved on through Blount County before lifting just south of Lake Guntersville. It was on the ground for 116 miles.

And, remember, this was the second tornado to strike Cordova on April 27, 2011. Odds of a small community like that being hit twice on the same day are extremely low.

CHAPTER 7: TUSCALOOSA/BIRMINGHAM

As the southern supercell moved into Tuscaloosa County, it was out of range of the camera in the field operated by Oldshue and Greer. We then changed the view of our SKYCAM atop the Tuscaloosa County Courthouse, pointed southwest, hoping to see something. Remember, most tornadoes in Alabama are rain-wrapped, and very difficult, if not impossible to see.

My colleague, Jason Simpson was operating the SKYCAM network and did a masterful job. I quickly went to a tornadic storm on the radar in northern Lamar County in West Alabama, but he asked me to take the Tuscaloosa camera because he had what he believed was the tornado in view. And, he was right. We stayed with the live video, mostly in a double box, for 17 minutes before we lost power. I had to use the double box since we had other tornadic storms that had to be covered in addition to the one approaching Tuscaloosa.

We have learned that people tend to take action without hesitation when they actually see a tornado through one of our cameras. But, when showing radar, they often just see what looks like a bucket of spilled paint, and even though we stress there is a very strong tornado signature, they wait until they can find some kind of visual confirmation. I know that Tuscaloosa SKYCAM live video was one of the most important parts of the coverage that day.

The ABC 33/40 SKYCAM network was born shortly after another violent tornado hit Tuscaloosa on December 16, 2000. At the time we had "towercams" on our various transmission towers across the state, and the controls for them were on the other side of the station's building, in the newsroom. On that day we had the EF-4 tornado on camera live, but it was a Saturday, nine days from Christmas, and we were short-staffed. The person running the camera really struggled, and we knew we needed something better.

The new SKYCAM network would feature a system that gave meteorologists full control from the weather office, including pan, tilt, and zoom capability, right in the weather office. It really paid off on that horrible April day in 2011 with historic video streams.

As the large tornado approached Tuscaloosa, I was struggling for the right words to say. Coming from an engineering and physical science background, I don't have a deep vocabulary. At one point, when Jason zoomed in on the tornado which showed a multiple vortex look with debris, I simply said…

"This will be a day that will go down in state history. And all you can do is pray for those people".

It was indeed a day that went down in state history. And, I honestly believe some took the time to pray.

The adrenaline was pumping; this thing was headed right for the middle of Tuscaloosa. But, understand we had 11 other Alabama counties under a tornado warning at the same time, and I had to cover them as well. Life is precious whether you live in Tuscaloosa or a smaller, rural town somewhere else in Alabama.

The Tuscaloosa EF-4 tornado, live on ABC 33/40 April 27, 2011. This SKYCAM is atop the Tuscaloosa County Courthouse.

We did spend most of the time on air for the next ten minutes covering the tornado approaching Tuscaloosa. We lost the camera briefly, but it came back as the tornado was moving into the city.

During the brief downtime I had to use radar exclusively, and I was crippled by an error in the graphics system that put the radar pixels about five miles south of the actual location. I had no idea at the time, and for a minute or so I was more concerned about Skyland Boulevard (south of the actual tornado track) than 15th Street (a main east-west corridor in Tuscaloosa that was the epicenter of the severe damage for a while).

Lesson learned: always have two radar sources when you are working a tornado event, not one. I have reason to believe that my use of the erroneous radar data for that brief time was responsible for the loss of life. While I don't play mental gymnastics with it, my mind does drift back to that situation occasionally. ALWAYS have two sources.

As the supercell moved east of Tuscaloosa, there was no time to think about what happened there. That same storm was moving in the direction of Birmingham, and we had to warn people there. Other tornadoes were moving through various parts of North and West Alabama. No rest for the weary.

In the coming hours, we started seeing the live video from our reporters in Tuscaloosa, and photos and video coming in from social media. It looked bad. Really bad. But you never really know the severity of the damage until the next morning, at the first light of day.

A couple of hours after the tornado moved through the city, a producer in my ear was telling me that Tuscaloosa Mayor Walt Maddox was on the phone, and wanted to speak with me on the air. I was under the assumption that he was going to give us an update on the damage and casualty count. But he was actually looking for weather information. Their operations center was damaged, and the communication ability was extremely limited. They heard another tornado was on the way and wanted an update. Of course, I provided him with the accurate information -- thankfully there was no second tornado.

As the tornado approached the Birmingham metro area, we had more cameras and live streams from the field looking at it. Unfortunately, the tornado had become mostly rain-wrapped and was not easy to see. But we all knew it was still there. And, it was going to impact some of the western and northern suburbs, not far from the path of an EF-5 tornado on April 8, 1998, that killed 32 people in the Birmingham area.

We continued to use the strongest wording possible. This was a true tornado emergency for the western and northern parts of the Birmingham metro. Get into a safe place NOW. Small room, lowest floor, near the center of the house, and away from windows. No cars, no mobile homes. It was wrapped in rain, but it was there, still producing extreme damage. The ominous hook and debris ball never went away.

For some, the illusion was that nothing happened in Birmingham because the downtown area was intact and didn't suffer any damage. But just to the northwest, the damage was severe, with loss of life, in communities like Concord, Pleasant Grove, Pratt City, and Fultondale.

The big tornado lifted just east of I-65, and just north of downtown Birmingham. But, the supercell would later produce another tornado east of Birmingham, moving through places like Shoal Creek Valley in St. Clair County, and Webster's Chapel in Calhoun County. The EF-4 stayed down into Northwest Georgia.

Just to the south of my TV market, another violent EF-4 tornado tore through parts of Elmore, Tallapoosa, and Chambers counties between 8:15 and 9:00p.m. CT. Right through scenic Lake Martin. This one killed seven people. The last tornado of the day in Alabama moved through southern Chilton County near Verbena shortly before 10:00p.m.

CHAPTER 8: SO MANY HEROES

When the last tornado warning was over and we pitched to our news team for an extended version of our 10:00p news to show all of the damage, there was a moment or two for me to gather my thoughts. Did this really happen? I just worked an event like the 1974 Superoutbreak that got me into this business. How many people have died? Was there a good response to the warnings? Were people paying attention? What can I do to help now?

I watched the various live reports from our field reporters who had been waiting patiently for our tornado coverage to end so they could tell stories of the humanitarian crisis and massive loss of property. It was dark, of course, and I knew the real story would not be known until daybreak the next day. But this was bad... really, really bad. There was a very significant loss of life.

Honestly, I can't recall much about my next day on April 28, 2011. As usual, I slept about 3 hours, if that much, before the morning shift from my home office started. Even after a historic weather day, the products and services I deliver must be produced and pushed out to the public. I did the morning "Weather Xtreme Video" as usual, wrote a blog post and discussion on weather expectations for the next seven to ten days, and did weather reports on the radio for about two dozen stations. Through all of this I tried to keep an eye on ABC 33/40's morning news to see what daylight would bring in the hardest hit areas. While writing this book, I pulled up my calendar for April 28, 2011, and saw no school visits. Most likely I had one scheduled and it was canceled due to damage or the lack of power. I do clearly recall speaking to the third graders at Calera Elementary on April 26, the day before the outbreak.

That same night, April 28, I did the early evening weather segments on ABC 33/40 live from Pleasant Grove, which was hit head-on by an EF-4 tornado (the same one that moved through Tuscaloosa about an hour earlier in the day). I found some time to walk around between the 5:00 and 6:00 newscasts. No matter how many times you see catastrophic damage from a tornado, it still takes your breath away. As far as the eye can see, nothing but flattened homes. As I walked through the neighborhood, I saw photos, teddy bears, trophies, pieces of furniture, and other items that represented so many lives shattered. I've seen it before, but never get used to it. Their world came apart in less than two minutes as the tornado passed through with winds of over 150 mph.

I am not sure if anyone was there from state or federal agencies, but I will never forget armies of locals, coming from parts of Pleasant Grove and other nearby communities not damaged, in the hardest hit areas and ministering to people. They were mostly church groups who were well organized and working hard, handing out food, working chainsaws, and praying for those who were hurting so badly. No paperwork to fill out, no red tape. Anyone in need was getting help from ordinary people who became unrecognized heroes. Most of them kept working until they suffered from soul exhaustion.

For me personally, there was no time to "get off the grid". Social media was coming of age, and the constant messages from those needing help just didn't stop across the various platforms... for days. My position after the tornado was pretty much that of a town crier. I would retweet and share urgent requests from those in need, turning my large social media followers into a pool of relief workers. The hashtags #needs and #haves were used.

There were so many heroes. In America today, you see so much hate, anger, rage, and vitriol. In the days and weeks following April 27, 2011, in Alabama, there was unity. People were unified in their effort to help their neighbors in need. Really didn't matter if they voted Democrat or Republican. If they were black or white. Pulled for Alabama or Auburn. Nobody even asked or cared, it was a remarkable effort of people helping people.

The national media was there for a day or two after the generational tornado outbreak, but the attention on this tragedy of historic proportions didn't last long. You see, the wedding of Prince William and Catherine Middleton took place two days later, on April 29, 2011 at Westminster Abbey. All of the networks and other national media outlets moved their attention from the tornado disaster to the royal wedding. I'm not blaming them; it is just what they do. But the bottom line is that most people in the nation know very little about the Alabama tornadoes of 2011 because the story just wasn't told. I would even suggest the horrible tornado that struck Joplin, Missouri, the next month on May 22 got much more national attention. Don't get me wrong; Joplin was a huge story and a terrible disaster with 158 fatalities from an EF-5 tornado. But, in Alabama on April 27, 2011, we dealt with 62 tornadoes (including 3 EF-5s) that killed 252 people.

I should add that losing 252 people from one single tornado event is inexcusable. For anyone in the weather enterprise, and for the people of Alabama. You see, those that died were precious people. Some were college students. Others were infants, senior adults, moms and dads. Many children died. Some lived in cities, others were far out in the country. It impacted just about every socioeconomic group.

Even the local journalists struggled to cover the Alabama tornadoes. Just too much to tell, no way you could cover what happened along the tracks of all 62 tornadoes. The vastness of the tragedy would not allow it. The point of this book is to share April 27, 2011 stories of ordinary people doing extraordinary things to help their neighbors. And more about some of the people who lost their lives that day, and those who survived.

I put out a call across my social media platforms in 2020, asking for suggestions on some of the stories that needed to be told. I was inundated, and the hardest part was determining which ones to share here in the book. For me, it was an emotionally draining experience going through all the responses. But, I understand I have no capacity to feel the real burden as those who lost loved ones, or survived a tornado encounter themselves that horrible day.

Know this is an incomplete collection of the pain, courage and perseverance experienced and displayed by the people of Alabama ten years ago. But it is an important collection of stories that need to be told. Let me stress again, I am no writer; I am a physical science guy. But it is an honor for me to put these words into this book. Future generations need to know about this day. Not only the science behind it all, but more importantly, the people we lost, and those who survived.

CHAPTER 9: SEVEN FAMILY MEMBERS IN THE BASEMENT; SIX SURVIVED

In April 2011, Carrie Lowe and her husband Josh were new parents living in Pleasant Grove. Their son, Tucker, was born in March, and Carrie was on maternity leave from her job as an emergency room nurse at St. Vincent's East.

Carrie's brother, Curt Grier, and his wife Crystal, lived just a couple of miles away, also in Pleasant Grove. Crystal describes Carrie as a person "that loved everybody, was a friend to all, and didn't have one enemy". She loved to help people.

Carrie and Josh Lowe with their newborn son Tucker

Carrie also paid close attention to the weather, especially when severe thunderstorms were forecast. Her last post on Twitter, one week before the big tornado outbreak on April 20, 2011, showed concern over getting the warnings that day due to a power outage.

Carrie Lowe
@carriegrierlowe

I hate bad weather. Hope someone warns me to go to my safe place if I need to cause the power is out so I can't watch James Spann. :(

11:51 PM · Apr 20, 2011 · TweetDeck

Carrie Lowe's last post on Twitter - April 20, 2011

Curt says Carrie had been afraid of tornadoes since she was a little girl. She had been talking about the April 27 threat for several days. The event was well forecast, and she paid close attention.

The morning round of storms on April 27 knocked out the power at a school in Bessemer, where Crystal's five year old daughter, Rachel, attended. Since Rachel was out of school, Crystal, her 10 month old son, Jacob, and Rachel went shopping. Upon returning to their home, Crystal realized she locked herself out of the house.

Knowing that Carrie had a spare key, Crystal called her for help. Carrie wasn't home, but was out with Josh, about to eat lunch in Bessemer. Lunch had to wait; they came right back to Pleasant Grove to let Crystal in. It was about that time that Curt got home; he worked for Birmingham Fire and Rescue.

They all decided to have a late lunch together, and headed for Speedy's in Hueytown, a great little Mexican restaurant. Knowing the significant severe weather threat that was ahead during the late afternoon and evening hours, Crystal invited Carrie, Josh, and Tucker over to their home so they could ride out the storms together. Carrie and Josh lived in a one level house; Crystal and Curt had a basement which was partially finished. It would seemingly offer better protection at 1320 12th Street.

The Grier home on 12th Street in Pleasant Grove on a snowy day in March 2009

Earlier in the week, Carrie's mom encouraged the Lowe family to ride out the storms at their home in Hayden, but Carrie assured her they would be safe at Crystal's house with a basement.

57

At the Grier home, they turned on the television and watched ABC 33/40's live coverage of the devastating tornado that was moving through Tuscaloosa shortly after 5:00 p.m. As the storm neared the western suburbs of Birmingham, including Pleasant Grove, rain intensities increased, and the satellite signal was lost at the Grier home.

At that time Carrie encouraged everyone to get to the basement, knowing what was to come. She put her baby, Tucker, in his car seat, and all seven people went down the stairs and into the basement. Carrie asked Crystal if she had her purse; that didn't make sense to Crystal, but Carrie said it would be helpful if she needed to be identified. Again, it seemed senseless to Crystal, especially since she really didn't think a tornado was coming.

Carrie opted to go into the part of the basement which is under the front porch of the home, not the finished part of the basement which featured a couch and other amenities. The other family members followed her into that long, but smaller space. With Carrie's son Tucker safe in the car seat, she offered to hold Crystal's son, Jacob.

After only about five minutes, the roaring noise of the wind picked up, and while Crystal's mom called to check on her. The roar got louder and louder and just as Crystal told her mom, "it's right on top of us," the phone went silent and the connection was dropped.

The rain wrapped EF-4 tornado moving through Pleasant Grove, as seen from atop Shades Mountain at Bluff Park. Photo from Michael D. Lawrence.

With all seven family members standing in that part of the basement under the porch, a violent, EF-4 tornado passed overhead. Large pieces of concrete started falling on top of them as the structure above disintegrated. All of this happened during a few seconds of nature's violence that cannot be adequately described by those that experience it.

When it was over, Crystal and Curt were uninjured, but they were under pieces of concrete block. Curt cleared the debris and they saw Josh, who was knocked down but not seriously injured. But, at that point they could not see Carrie or the three kids. Curt started yelling out their names, and there was no response. Nothing. Crystal, Curt, and Josh feared the worst.

The long slab of concrete that had been the ceiling of the portion of the basement, fell and broke into a few large pieces. One came down over Carrie and Jacob. Rachel and Tucker, in the car seat, were adjacent to the other three in the basement.

This is where all seven family members were huddled together during the EF-4 tornado in Pleasant Grove at 1320 12th Street

Curt, a trained firefighter, was able to get behind the large concrete slab and saw Carrie's arm. He immediately felt her pulse; and he knew his sister was gone. And, from all evidence, she died while covering and protecting Jacob. As Curt called out for Jacob, the ten month old child crawled out despite having a skull fracture. Curt picked up Jacob and handed him to Crystal.

Then, Curt started working to find out the condition of Rachel and Tucker, who was in the car seat. Another large chunk of concrete had fallen on both of them; Curt was able to determine the baby survived in that car seat, but there was a considerable amount of debris in his mouth. Curt was able to reach around the slab and clear the baby's mouth to be sure he was able to breathe normally. Rachel started screaming, asking someone to get the large piece of concrete off of her. While terrifying, the screams gave everyone some level of comfort knowing she was alive.

By this time neighbors, ordinary people who did extraordinary things that horrible night, showed up to help. It would take first responders a considerable amount of time to reach the house because of all the downed trees, debris, and live power lines.

At least ten men from the street tried their best to lift the large concrete slab off of Carrie and Rachel with no luck. It was just too heavy. For the neighbors who still had homes, they rushed back to get jacks out of their cars. It worked; about six or seven jacks were put under the big slab, and it slowly started to rise, allowing for Rachel to be rescued. Rachel had head injuries, but she was alert and talking.

Neighbors trying to lift large pieces of concrete covering those trapped in the basement at the Grier home the evening of April 27, 2011

Curt knew that the three children needed medical attention, and there was no telling how long it could take for paramedics to arrive. Their cars were taken out by the tornado, so a neighbor handed them her keys and told them where to find her car. It was located at the end of 12th Street that was untouched by the tornado. Curt and Crystal carried Rachel and Jacob. A neighbor carried Tucker, as Josh stayed behind with Carrie.

Unfortunately the car didn't offer much help; downed trees had roads blocked and there was simply no passage until chainsaw crews arrived. They started walking again. Then, a neighbor on a golf cart offered a ride, but that again didn't last long due to fallen trees. After another long walk, they found a police officer that gave them a ride down to one of the local fire stations, where a triage setup had been established.

From there, the children were transported to Children's Hospital of Alabama.

Back at 1320 12th Street, the volunteers were finally able to get the concrete slab off Carrie. Chris Coleman, who was a nurse at Children's of Alabama, was determined to save Carrie's life. She performed CPR on her for an extended amount of time. Unfortunately, Carrie passed away from her injuries.

The irony in all of this was that Carrie and Josh's home was not damaged at all.

Crystal and Curt opted not to rebuild in Pleasant Grove; they moved to Blount County after the tornado. Josh and Tucker moved in with the Grier family for a couple of years; Crystal quit her job temporarily so she could take care of the kids. Josh remarried and has added two more children to his growing family.

**The Grier residence in Pleasant Grove after the
4.27.11 EF-4 tornado**

Jacob's skull fractures healed on their own. Rachel suffered a brachial plexus injury leaving her left arm paralyzed. Crystal and Curt were told she had one nerve working in her arm from her neck to her fingers and would need surgery that would only give her sixty percent use. One Sunday about three months after the tornado, the Grier's pastor called her up for prayer in church and anointed her with oil. She regained full use of her arm about a week later and still has no issues to this day. The medical team called it a miracle.

Carrie's seven week old baby, Tucker, is now ten years old. When he was 18 months old he was diagnosed with a rare genetic disorder, Tetrasomy 9p, but he is thriving.

Crystal Grier and Tucker Lowe, Carrie's son

Crystal and Curt had another son the next year, Ethan Lee. The nurse that performed CPR on Carrie, trying to save her life, told Crystal her son's name was Ethan. Ethan and his friends joined hands the night of April 27 to pray over Carrie during the rescue. And, Lee was Carrie's middle name.

Ethan was born on January 23, 2012, almost 9 months to the day after the April 27 tornado outbreak. And, there were tornadoes on that day. A pre-dawn tornado tore through Center Point and Clay, killing 16 year old Christina Heichelbech, and injuring 75.

Curt, a Birmingham firefighter, worked in that area; Crystal wasn't sure if he would make it in time for the birth, but he did. They call Ethan their tornado baby, and in the words of Crystal, "he helped heal our family."

Curt and Crystal Grier, their daughter Rachel, and sons Jacob and Ethan

Crystal has what they call the family "tornado box" which is full of cards sent by friends and others, newspaper articles, and photos. On April 27, 2020, Crystal believed that Jacob, now 10, was old enough to hear the entire story of that horrible night ten years ago. She read a number of the articles to him, and told him how Carrie protected him and saved his life.

Josh Lowe has remarried, and now Tucker has a brother and sister, Matthew and Harper.

Josh and Laurel Lowe, and their children Tucker, Harper, and Matthew

Reflecting back on April 27, 2011, Crystal remembered that the long space under the porch had a left and a right side. Carrie led everyone into the right side that had some things stored in it instead of the other side that was completely clear. If they had gone to the left side, it probably would have killed all seven people because the slabs were bigger and didn't break up like they did on the right side. It was like Carrie knew something the other family members didn't, and Crystal believes they are here today because of her. She just wishes Carrie could have saved herself as well.

For Crystal, this night changed her life completely. For one, Carrie is not here. They were sisters-in-law, they were also best friends. They were supposed to live near each other for the rest of their lives and raise their kids together. When Carrie took Jacob from Crystal's arms and carried him downstairs, it was the last time the family saw her. The slab that hit her was very large, and Crystal didn't see her before they got her out. Crystal says it feels like this left them with no closure. So many things remind Crystal of her, and that always brings her mind back to the last time she saw her. Carrie's mom passed away in 2019. These were the kinds of things their family wasn't supposed to experience without Carrie, just like every birthday, holiday, or celebration.

Crystal is thankful to say that the Lord has sustained them through it all. One of Carrie's favorite verses was Joshua 1:9:

Have I not commanded you? Be strong and courageous. Do not be afraid; do not be discouraged, for the Lord your God will be with you wherever you go.

To this day Crystal and her family don't understand it all, but they know, "He is with us wherever we go." She used to think that meant wherever they physically went. Now she realizes it is also through grief, sorrow, and sadness.

CHAPTER 10: THREE LIVES SPARED;
ALL ELSE GONE

For me, the foothills of the Appalachians in Northeast Alabama are a retreat. Clearly one of the most beautiful parts of our state, it offers stunning beauty year-round, especially during the fall when brilliant colors make the hillsides come alive. A winding drive down country roads in counties like Jackson, DeKalb, and Marshall is good for the soul. It is only about 80 miles from Birmingham, but you feel like you are a million miles away.

Nestled in the northeast corner of Alabama is the community of Bridgeport in Jackson County. The town was developed after the 1840s, when European Americans established a riverboat landing along the Tennessee River. A railroad bridge over the Tennessee River was completed in 1854, connecting the city with nearby Chattanooga, Tennessee. In recognition of this accomplishment, the name of the city was changed from Jonesville to "Bridgeport."

Hollie Beasley, along with her husband Kevin and their two-year old son Talon, lived at 1291 County Road 255 in Bridgeport on April 27, 2011. Kevin and Talon were home, and Hollie went to work in Scottsboro that morning at an attorney's office. Later in the day, the attorney that Hollie worked for was leaving the office for the courthouse as he had a case scheduled in court. A line of storms was approaching so he asked her to go with him to the courthouse so that she wouldn't be in the office alone. They knew this was a major severe weather threat, not to be taken lightly. They waited out the thunderstorm in the judge's chambers; and after that storm passed, he told Hollie to go home before the next round arrived.

The Beasley's home in Bridgeport in April 2011

Hollie was able to make it home and Talon was napping. They had satellite television service, which went out due to rain attenuation. Hollie's mom called a few minutes before 5:00 p.m. to let her know meteorologists on Huntsville TV stations were watching a dangerous storm moving in the direction of Bridgeport. The storm was rotating, had an intense velocity couplet developed on radar, and a tornado warning was being issued for the northeast part of Jackson County.

```
BULLETIN - EAS ACTIVATION REQUESTED
TORNADO WARNING
NATIONAL WEATHER SERVICE HUNTSVILLE AL
500 PM CDT WED APR 27 2011

THE NATIONAL WEATHER SERVICE IN HUNTSVILLE HAS ISSUED A

* TORNADO WARNING FOR...
  NORTHEASTERN JACKSON COUNTY IN NORTHEAST ALABAMA...

* UNTIL 530 PM CDT

* AT 457 PM CDT...NATIONAL WEATHER SERVICE DOPPLER RADAR INDICATED A
  SEVERE THUNDERSTORM CAPABLE OF PRODUCING A TORNADO NEAR
  HOLLYWOOD MOVING NORTHEAST AT 75 MPH.

* LOCATIONS NEAR THE PATH OF THIS TORNADO INCLUDE...
  STEVENSON.
  RUSSELL CAVE NATIONAL MONUMENT.
  BRIDGEPORT.

PRECAUTIONARY/PREPAREDNESS ACTIONS...

TAKE COVER NOW! MOVE TO AN INTERIOR ROOM ON THE LOWEST FLOOR OF A
STURDY BUILDING. AVOID WINDOWS. IF IN A MOBILE HOME...A VEHICLE OR
OUTDOORS...MOVE TO THE CLOSEST SUBSTANTIAL SHELTER AND PROTECT
YOURSELF FROM FLYING DEBRIS.
```

**Tornado warning issued at 5pm CT
April 27, 2011, for Jackson County**

Hollie woke Talon and put him in the bathtub on top of a few pillows in only a t-shirt and diaper. Kevin pulled a mattress into the bathroom in case it became necessary to use for cover. Hollie, in her pajamas and no shoes, was in the bathroom with Talon and yelled for Kevin to come as the wind was picking up. She couldn't hear him, so she left the bathroom and found him at the back door. On the way back to the bathroom, they looked out the front door and could see the dark clouds swirling.

Hollie ran to the bathroom to prepare for the worst. Moments later Kevin came running into the bathroom and pulled the mattress over the top of them just in time to hear the vinyl siding being ripped off their 3-year-old home. Hollie remembers feeling the bathtub shifting side to side before she lost consciousness.

Her first memory after the tornado was being in their yard approximately 50 yards from where she was inside their home. Kevin was 6 feet to her left and Talon was 6 feet to her right. She can vividly remember the sound of Talon saying, "mommy, mommy" over and over. With that sound, she gained a little relief just by hearing his voice and knowing he was alive. Kevin ran to him and picked him up as best he could while Hollie lifted herself off the ground, nauseous and dizzy. Kevin quickly asked her if she was able to carry Talon because he could barely breathe and had severe pain in his chest and lower back.

The Beasley's home site on April 28, 2011

They were able to walk to their neighbor's house crossing over downed power lines and trees while wearing no shoes. The neighbor's home was also demolished, but they had taken cover in their basement, a move that caused them to receive no injuries and be able to help the Beasley family. Other neighbors who received no damage came to assist in getting them to the nearest home that was still intact. They carried Kevin into that house and laid him on the couch to hopefully get some relief from the pain. The ambulance couldn't get to them because of all the downed trees blocking the road.

Hollie's car in this field was lofted and thrown from their driveway during the tornado

Their neighbors managed to get a pick-up truck to the Beasley family and put couch cushions in the bed of the truck. They were able to get Kevin onto the cushions while Talon and Hollie rode up front. They transported them to the ambulance which then took them to Highlands Medical Center in Scottsboro, where they were operating on generators. Thankfully, Hollie personally knew the security officer at the hospital; he was waiting for their arrival at the emergency room doors. He immediately let her know that he had already contacted her parents and let them know that they needed to get to the hospital. When her parents arrived, they didn't know what had happened. They thought they were in a car accident because a tornado in Bridgeport hadn't been reported at the time. Many people today don't know anything about the EF-4 in Bridgeport that almost took the lives of the Beasley family. However, that horrible night it did take the life of a 13-year-old boy that lived across the street, Branen Warren.

Many tests were done on Hollie, Kevin, and Talon. Hollie was bruised from head-to-toe but had no major issues. Talon had a skull fracture and was quickly transferred to T C Thompson Children's Hospital in Chattanooga as Highlands didn't have the necessary machinery to assess the severity of the skull fracture due to the power outage. Thankfully since Hollie was without any major issues, she was able to ride along with Talon from Scottsboro to Chattanooga. Her parents arrived in Chattanooga not long after them with a change of clothes, hairbrush and a pair of shoes for Hollie. Once Talon was admitted and settled into a pediatric ICU room, Hollie's mom stayed in the room with him and she was able to take a bath in one of the unoccupied rooms and change out of the muddy clothes she was wearing. It was a difficult bath as she was so sore all over and there was no hot water. She remembers all the dirt and grass that came out of her hair. Kevin sustained two fracture vertebrae and a fractured sternum, so he was unable to join them in Chattanooga as he remained at Highlands to receive treatment.

A few days later, they were all released from both hospitals and went to stay with family who, without hesitation, gave them a place to live for a few months. The Beasley family was so thankful to the many friends and families who helped them get back on their feet. The outpouring of love and generosity was simply astonishing to them.

After the storm and damage assessment, there was nothing left of their home. There was no piece of the bathtub that they were in, not a single piece of their California King-sized bedroom suite, no kitchen appliances, no living room furniture, and not one wall remaining. Their vehicles were totaled and thrown yards from where they were originally parked. An 18-wheeler was thrown from across the street into their yard, not far from where Talon was thrown. While nothing remained of their first home, Hollie's engagement ring and Kevin's wallet were found in a cinderblock where the foundation of their home had once stood.

It took some time, but they all recovered. These days, storms have become a little easier to deal with, but high wind is something that still gets to the Beasley family. They might have lost all the material things they owned that terrifying day, but their lives were spared. Everything else can be, and was, replaced.

A week or so after the April 27, 2011 tornado outbreak, there was a Facebook page created to find owners of items that fell from the sky and landed in people's yards across the Deep South. One of Hollie's friends saw a post with a photo of Hollie and Talon, and ultimately the photo was returned to the family. This picture was taken when Talon was 4 months old. It was ripped from his baby book and landed in a yard 56 miles away in Pikeville, Tennessee.

**This photo of Hollie and Talon traveled
56 miles in the tornado**

In 2012, Kevin and Hollie needed new family pictures since all of the old ones were taken from them during the tornado. The decision was made to go back to their old home site on County Road 255. It was their first time going back to the place where they almost lost their lives. They chose not to rebuild there; they didn't want to have to look at the area every day and be constantly reminded of what happened.

Hollie, Talon, and Kevin in 2012, at the site of their home that was destroyed

Hollie still sometimes wonders "why us?" There have been many great things that have happened to the family since that horrific day in 2011, and also obstacles that this terrifying day have given them the strength to overcome. The past ten years have allowed Talon to grow up and become a smart, handsome young man and also allowed Hollie and Kevin to add a little girl to their family. Tenlie Kate was born on January 31, 2019.

Talon and Tenlie Kate Beasley

Talon is 12 years old now and he is kind, loving and thoughtful. He wants to be an anesthesiologist when he grows up. Hollie and Kevin are hopeful that one day his life being spared on April 27, 2011, will allow his kind, nurturing spirit to be used for an amazing purpose however God sees fit. Kevin and Hollie have since taken great jobs and have been very successful. Their children have everything they need and more. Most importantly, their children have their parents.

On April 27, 2018, they finally made something positive out of April 27th - Kevin and Hollie closed on and moved into their dream home in the Hollywood community of Jackson County, about 20 miles away from Bridgeport.

Talon, Hollie, Kevin, and Tenlie Kate Beasley in 2020

Hollie received her real estate license in April 2020. This is something she had wanted to do for a long time; she sold six homes in her first six months, and loves seeing her clients' faces when they close on their dream homes. Hollie says it is nice for her to be a part of such a special day in others' lives. She only hopes she can make a small difference in the lives of those around her.

CHAPTER 11: SHE WAS SMILING

Michael and Tina Forrest moved from Nashville to Alabama in 1996. Michael worked for a company called Nashville Electrographics, which printed magazines like Southern Living and Cooking Light. They opened a facility in Birmingham, and Michael was asked to make the move to be in charge of the new location.

With Tina taking a job as a paralegal in Rainbow City, the family decided to move to Lake Neely Henry in Ohatchee. It was a beautiful property on Eagle Cove Road just off Alabama Highway 77; a horse pasture was across the way along with the 5W Ranch which offers hydrotherapeutic exercise for horses.

Michael and Tina Forrest

The Great Recession in 2008 brought a career change for Michael; he took a job with Publix, working at the same store (Lee Branch, off U.S. 280 in northern Shelby

County) as his daughter, Jessica Peterson, who worked in the bakery. Michael was a "people person", and he absolutely loved his new job, stocking the shelves and helping guests find what they needed.

Michael Forrest and his granddaughter Ariel

In 2011, Michael and Tina's son Blake was in the Marines and stationed in Afghanistan. During his first few years of military training he stayed with his parents in Ohatchee when he was able to take leave. The Afghanistan tour of duty was a long one, and after being there for a year

Blake was scheduled to arrive back at Camp Lejeune on May 4, 2011. Michael, Tina, and Jessica came up with a plan to go to North Carolina and surprise Blake upon his arrival back in the States. Tina was to make the drive first, then Michael and Jessica would come the next day after work. Afghanistan was a very dangerous place, and to the Forrest family it was a miracle in their eyes that Blake was returning safely.

Exactly one week before Blake was scheduled to arrive back in the States, on April 27, Jessica had a typical day planned. She went to work in the Publix bakery, and Michael was on duty that day as well. Jessica noticed many of the guests in the store talking about the potential for severe thunderstorms and tornadoes, but she didn't have much time to think about it. After their shift ended, Jessica invited her dad to stay with her family in their Vestavia apartment that night. He would spend the night there often when he was working consecutive days so he wouldn't have to make the long drive to Ohatchee, a 60-mile drive.

But on this day, Michael decided to make the drive back home to Lake Neely Henry because he wanted to be with Tina. Michael and Jessica hugged, told each other "I love you", and they went their separate ways.

Once home, Jessica, her husband James, and 4-year-old daughter Ariel opted to watch a movie together. During the movie, Jessica received a text from her mom in Ohatchee asking if they were okay; Tina was watching weather coverage and was concerned. Jessica told Tina they were all fine and enjoying a family movie night together. Unfortunately Jessica had no idea a violent tornado was down in St. Clair County and was headed directly toward her parents' home on Eagle Cove Road on the lake. The Peterson family went to bed that night with no knowledge of the violent tornadoes that were tearing through Alabama.

The next day, April 28, Jessica got up and headed for work. Like every day, she started whipping up cakes and sweets in the Publix Bakery. She noticed most people were making comments about the tornadoes in Alabama the day before and how the death toll was climbing. Jessica and her family were pretty much "off the grid" and weren't aware of the tragedy. At one point that morning she received a call from some extended family members in Tennessee asking if she had heard from her parents.

At the time, Jessica didn't give it much thought. She told them the power was probably out, and they couldn't charge their phones. Jessica right away tried calling them herself, but got no answer. A few hours went by and still no word. This is when fear crept into Jessica's mind. Were they close to a tornado? Were they hurt? Could they be in a hospital being treated for injuries from the storm? Even at this point it never crossed her mind that they could have possibly lost their lives.

While Jessica was waiting to hear from her parents in Ohatchee, she called her husband James, who wanted to drive over to the lake to check on Michael and Tina. Instead, Jessica told him to call the local police or fire department for information. She knew there could probably be trees down everywhere and making that drive would be almost impossible.

After that phone call, thoughts were swirling in Jessica's mind. She told a friend in the Publix that if by some crazy chance Michael and Tina were killed by a tornado, it would be horrible, but at the same time it would be okay because of their faith.

A few moments later a coworker in the bakery answered the phone, and Jessica could tell by the sound of the conversation something was wrong. Later Jessica would find out the person on the phone was her husband James, who told the coworker that Michael had died in a tornado, Tina was missing, and he was on the way to the Publix.

As James walked into the store, Jessica was called up to meet him. At that point he grabbed Jessica's hand, looked her in the eyes, and before he would say a word, she knew what would follow. James could barely get the words out. Michael was dead, Tina was missing. A horrible tornado had come right down Eagle Cove Road.

For Jessica, her world exploded in that brief moment. Her grief was overwhelming and unbearable. But within seconds she immediately thought about her brother Blake. How in the world would they tell him? He would be home in one week.

After calling family in Tennessee, Jessica and James jumped in the car and made their way up I-59 towards Gadsden Regional Medical Center. After the tornado, a neighbor found Michael floating in Lake Neely Henry behind their house. He was responsive, but had suffered a blow to the back of the head and wasn't speaking clearly. The only words from his mouth were about his wife. An ambulance was finally able to get through the debris and took him to the hospital in Gadsden. The clinicians did everything possible, but Michael died that night due to severe head trauma and being impaled from debris. The nurses told James and Jessica that Michael was peaceful when he passed away.

At the hospital, Jessica was told that Michael didn't have any identification, and she needed to identify the body. Jessica, James, and their pastor Frankie Powell all walked together to a room in the hospital. For Jessica, it was beyond surreal. Yesterday, she was working with her dad, and tonight she was identifying his body in a hospital? How could this happen?

They walked into the room and saw a blue blanket covering a body. Jessica was having a hard time believing this was actually happening. James grabbed Jessica's shoulders, and they pulled back the blanket to reveal Michael's face. At that moment, Jessica said, "this is just my dad's body, a vessel, his spirit is with the Lord". Michael looked so peaceful, which gave the family comfort as well. You see, Michael never feared death because he knew he was heaven-bound.

But this night was far from over; Tina was still missing. James and Jessica left the hospital in Gadsden and drove down Highway 77 toward their property on Lake Neely Henry in Ohatchee. As they arrived, it looked as though a bomb had been dropped on the neighborhood. They got close to Eagle Cove Road, but had to walk a ways because of the downed trees, power lines, and the debris. It was hard to recognize anything.

Jessica and James pretty much knew that Tina was gone, but they wanted to be able to bury her. They finally got to their driveway, and that was all that was left. A driveway. The house was lifted off the foundation and mostly disintegrated. Part of the front porch remained, and that was it. The site was beyond shocking.

The next day Tina's body was found by a dive team in Lake Neely Henry, pinned under a tree in the lake. The members of that dive team worked all through the night, and found her the next day, on April 28.

Jessica never realized how much of a blessing it was to just be able to go through her parent's things and find those memories that are connected to tangible items. After a search of their property and the neighborhood, Jessica and James walked away with a small handful of items; everything else... gone. She found a jacket her dad wore constantly with "Christ" monogrammed on it, her mom's Bible, a bottle of wine she made, and a metal cross that was slightly bent. They also found a football pin and a cross bracelet. James walked to the other side of the lake and found a few photo albums floating in the water. With some special care, they were able to salvage the photos... that was it.

The next day James and Jessica went shopping for clothes because they had nothing suitable in which to bury Michael and Tina. Jessica made sure she bought a cross necklace because her mom had quite the collection and always wore a different one every day to match her ensemble. The only piece of jewelry her mom had on when she was found was a dog tag bracelet Blake had made for her. She never took it off. She prayed for him constantly and the bracelet was a reminder of her unfailing commitment to pray unceasingly for those she loved.

A few days later Blake finally made it home; his commanding officer had already given him the news that his parents were killed in a tornado. He not only lost his parents, but his home and his belongings. He moved in with Jessica and James for the following year while he sorted out his new life as best he could.

Jessica's uncle Steven, Michael's brother, came and helped plan the arrangements for the Celebration of Life service. They chose to do that instead of a typical funeral because Tina always said she wanted them to celebrate their entrance into Heaven and not dwell on the fact they were gone. Easier said than done, but the request was honored by the family.

Jessica never actually saw her mom until the day before the funeral. She had to see her dad to identify him, but since her mom had her bracelet on, the dive team was able to determine it was her based on that one item. The funeral director asked Jessica if she wanted to see her, since the family decided to do a closed casket service.

After much debate in mind, she decided she would regret it for the rest of her life if she didn't. James, and Jessica's uncle and aunt, walked with her down the long hallway that led to the room where they saw Tina for the final time. Jessica can only describe what she saw next as being a gift from God because it gave her so much peace. Jessica approached her mom and looked at her face. She was smiling! In fact her smile was so big she was almost showing teeth. Jessica was floored. All four family members started to laugh because they had never seen that in their lives. It brought Jessica joy and peace to know that in the last moment of her mom's life when her whole world was coming down around her, she still smiled. She always wondered what Tina saw in that last moment, but Jessica is convinced it was Jesus welcoming her home with open arms.

Jessica says her faith has pulled her out of the darkest moments of her life. This was at the top of her list, but she says God is always faithful even after such a tragedy. Blake's Marine Corps. family showed up two days after he got home and cleaned up the property on Eagle Cove Road. Free meals were given to family members from the community while they sorted out details. The funeral home only charged half of the normal rate as a blessing. Publix paid for the flowers and fed the whole family while they were in town. A fund was created to pay for hotels and travel expenses so the extended family could afford to be there with the family. Jessica says she still has random moments of missing her parents horribly, but she says she is only temporarily separated from them; this life is but a vapor.

CHAPTER 12: THE NIGHT THAT NEVER ENDED

Travis Parker was Chief of Tuscaloosa Fire and Rescue Emergency Medical Services (EMS) in 2011. On April 27, after getting off work at 4:30 p.m. he was headed to pick up his children from his mother-in-law's home. Before he got there, he looked to the west and saw something he won't soon forget. A large tornado was visible, and in his words, "it was tearing Tuscaloosa up".

He knew he had to get back to work, and his route was up Alabama Highway 69, approaching Tuscaloosa from the south. By the time Travis got to the I-359 intersection, the tornado had already come through. He carefully drove through the debris field along I-359, but couldn't exit onto 15th Street. He went north to Jack Warner Parkway and headed east.

From radio communication, Parker learned that a crew was on the scene at Rosedale Court, where the damage was severe, and another crew was on 15th Street, also in the direct path of the tornado. At that time, the greatest need was for help in Alberta City, which was in ruins. He was able to turn north onto 25th Avenue and get into the area that desperately needed help.

Travis Parker told me it looked "like a bomb had gone off". He could not identify the location of Tuscaloosa Fire Station 4 in Alberta City; the community was unrecognizable. And soon after his arrival, he discovered three people who had just lost their lives in the tornado. They were Jackie Jefferson, 45, and two of her grandchildren, Cedria Harris, 9, and Keyshawn Harris, 5.

Parker covered their bodies and went to help establish a command center nearby.

Alberta City was unrecognizable for days after the April 27, 2011 tornado. Photo from James Spann.

Darkness was setting in, and with no power there were no street lights, no business lights. Pitch black. At the command center, firefighters turned on a large light on their truck to illuminate the parking lot where they were located. Parker tells me that people from all over Alberta City, who were able to walk, gravitated toward that light.

Some were injured, some homeless, some just wanted to know what was going to happen next.

TDOT (the Tuscaloosa Department of Transportation) was able to clear University Boulevard, enabling EMS team members to transport the injured to DCH Regional Medical Center and also the DCH Hospital in Northport.

The job was an all-nighter for Parker and his crew. He said they were simply too busy to think about the magnitude of the disaster, and emotion never came into play. They just did their jobs. Treating the injured, getting them to a hospital, and giving people the comforting knowledge that help was on the scene.

Robin Earley was on duty as a paramedic on April 27, 2011, working in an ambulance based in Walker County. She would be involved in the aftermath of five of the 62 tornadoes that day and night.

Her first assignment of the day was a medical transport (not related to the tornado outbreak) from Jasper to Princeton Baptist Medical Center in Birmingham. But as the day wore on, the calls became more frequent and chaotic. Earley and her crew were dispatched to Cullman to assist, and from there it was back to Walker County to help with the tornado injuries that had passed through Cordova. On the journey back to Walker County, debris was falling from the air, hitting the ambulance as it was traveling down Alabama Highway 69.

They made it to the Argo community, where they transported one injured patient to Birmingham. This started a "non-stop shuffle" that lasted for nearly 30 hours. During that time, Earley transported 22 patients to various hospitals in Birmingham. On one call, there was a family of five in the back of the ambulance.

A number of the 22 patients came from Pleasant Grove. Many of the injured were brought to the ambulance staging area on doors; it was the only way to keep the patients stabilized since they had run out of supplies.

A home in Pleasant Grove destroyed by the EF-4 tornado. Photo from Mandi French, who is seen in the photo on crutches. She survived in that house.

Earley described April 27 as "the best day of my career". Every patient they saw needed them. Nobody was taking advantage of the system; there was an urgent need for the services she could provide. She knew after that long night she made the right career decision.

I asked her about the nature of the injuries they saw that night. It was mostly blunt force trauma. Many had injuries to their feet; this is why we ask people to wear hard sole shoes when they are in a tornado warning polygon. Many had severe lacerations along with back and neck pain.

She says she wasn't tired during her 30-hour marathon; like Travis Parker, there simply wasn't enough time to think about the magnitude of the disaster or the scope of human suffering. It was all business.

It was a night when everyone in EMS worked together, according to Earley. That long, long night was their finest hour.

I have heard some people call meteorologists "heroes" after April 27, 2011. That is kind of someone to say, but it isn't true. The heroes were the first responders in the field that jumped into action. And, not just the professionals like Travis Parker and Robin Earley. Friends, relatives, neighbors rushing to help those around them in a dark, chaotic scene that most can't begin to imagine.

After my experience in the small hospital in Jasper in 1974, I know a little about what the first responders saw on April 27, 2011. I just hope they all know how much they are appreciated.

CHAPTER 13: ONE TOWN, TWO TORNADOES

Cordova is a small community in Walker County, about 40 miles northwest of Birmingham. The population in 2010 was 2,095; a place small enough where most folks know each other by name, or in some cases by reputation. The hub of the town is Cordova High School, home of the Blue Devils. The football team won state championships in 1995 and 2007. The boys' basketball team won the Class 4A state championship in 2018, becoming the first team in Walker County ever to do so.

The town sits on the Mulberry Fork of the Black Warrior River, and got the name "Cordova" by Captain Benjamin M. Long in 1859. He named the city after a city in Mexico where he was stationed during the Mexican–American War.

Many in this town are people of faith; the city has ten churches of multiple denominations. There is hope that growth will come to the community after the completion of Interstate 22, just to the southwest.

Severe thunderstorms and tornadoes are nothing new to the people of Walker County. At least 50 tornadoes have touched down across the county since 1950, including many strong/violent ones. During the Superoutbreak of April 3, 1974, downtown Jasper, the county seat, was hit head-on by a long-track EF-4 tornado.

On May 6, 2009, a tornado touched down on the west side of Cordova along South Street. The tornado moved through the heart of town and lifted shortly after it crossed near the intersection of Disney Street and Mass Avenue...near Cane Creek. Numerous trees were snapped off or were uprooted along the path; at least 15 homes were damaged by the fallen trees. One of the trees fell on a train and damaged some of the cars but the train did not derail. Thankfully, in this case, there were no deaths or injuries.

But on April 27, 2011, this community would deal with not just one, but two tornadoes in a 24-hour period; a day of destruction and human heartache.

Shortly after 5:15 a.m. that Wednesday, an EF-3 tornado, the first of the day, touched down near Franklin Ferry Road in the far southwest part of Walker County It crossed Alabama Highway 269 a mile or so south of Parrish, and would move through the heart of Cordova around 5:30a.m. In Cordova, the tornado caused significant damage to brick buildings in the downtown area. Trees were down on homes, and the entire community lost power. Along the 19-mile path in Walker County, this tornado was responsible for 20 injuries, most of them minor.

Fifteen-year-old Megan Johnson was at her home with her mom Julie that morning on Riceton Road, which is just east of the heart of Cordova. Her dad, Malcolm, was just getting off the third shift at American Cast Iron Pipe Company in Birmingham and wasn't home.

Megan, Malcolm, and Julie Johnson

Julie Johnson says when she heard me talking about the potential of a "generational event" on ABC 33/40 Friday, April 22, her antennae went up immediately. Of course, she had no way of knowing two tornadoes would move over their property, but she knew she had to be ready for whatever happened that day.

The early morning tornado passed within a quarter of a mile of their double-wide mobile home; the roof was damaged, and their trampoline went flying. Megan and Julie heard the tornado warning, while they were in the storm shelter on their property. Their shelter is one you see all across the Alabama countryside: made of cinder-blocks built into the side of a hill. Most of them have been around for decades. And, they work very well.

There was no major damage to their home, but power was lost during the storm, and service remained out for the rest of the day.

Megan was a tenth grader at Cordova High School, but on April 27, 2011, she stayed home since school was canceled due to the morning tornado, and the threat of additional severe weather later.

After the initial round of storms, the weather calmed by mid-morning. Sunshine returned and temperatures warmed nicely. Malcolm, after returning home from the third shift at ACIPCO, got some sleep, but said the day was so nice he would rather be fishing or playing golf. Despite the midday sun, the family was paying attention to the weather situation and knew more severe storms would likely develop by mid to late afternoon.

The Johnson family had a small battery-powered television in the kitchen and were watching ABC 33/40's live coverage of the Cullman tornado that afternoon while the sky was still blue over Cordova. That video brought more anxiety to the family of three and their "houseful of dogs"; nerves were frayed already after the morning tornado.

Malcolm went to get more gas for a small generator that was running at the house and Megan and Julie cleaned out the storm shelter, anticipating more severe weather. While this was happening, at 3:40 p.m., a tornado touched down in Pickens County in West Alabama near the community of Pickensville. Most in Cordova had no idea that tornado, at a straight-line distance of 73 miles to the southwest, would wind up moving right over their community again in about 80 minutes.

```
BULLETIN - EAS ACTIVATION REQUESTED
TORNADO WARNING
NATIONAL WEATHER SERVICE BIRMINGHAM AL
400 PM CDT WED APR 27 2011

THE NATIONAL WEATHER SERVICE IN BIRMINGHAM HAS ISSUED A

* TORNADO WARNING FOR...
  SOUTHERN FAYETTE COUNTY IN WEST CENTRAL ALABAMA...
  NORTHEASTERN PICKENS COUNTY IN WEST CENTRAL ALABAMA...
  NORTHWESTERN TUSCALOOSA COUNTY IN WEST CENTRAL ALABAMA...
  WALKER COUNTY IN CENTRAL ALABAMA...

* UNTIL 500 PM CDT

* AT 356 PM CDT...STORM SPOTTERS AND THE NATIONAL WEATHER SERVICE
  WERE TRACKING A LARGE AND EXTREMELY DANGEROUS TORNADO NEAR REFORM.
  DOPPLER RADAR SHOWED THIS TORNADO MOVING NORTHEAST AT 55 MPH.

* THE TORNADO WILL BE NEAR...
  BERRY AND BANKSTON AROUND 425 PM CDT.
  BOLEY SPRINGS AROUND 430 PM CDT.
  OAKMAN AROUND 440 PM CDT.
  PARRISH AROUND 445 PM CDT.
  JASPER AND CORDOVA AROUND 450 PM CDT.
  LYNNS PARK...SIPSEY AND CURRY AROUND 455 PM CDT.

OTHER LOCATIONS IMPACTED BY THE TORNADO INCLUDE MOORES BRIDGE...NEW
LEXINGTON...WEST CORONA...CORONA...GAMBLE AND MANCHESTER.

PRECAUTIONARY/PREPAREDNESS ACTIONS...

TO REPEAT...A LARGE...EXTREMELY DANGEROUS AND POTENTIALLY DEADLY
TORNADO IS ON THE GROUND. TO PROTECT YOUR LIFE...TAKE COVER NOW. FOR
YOUR PROTECTION MOVE TO AN INTERIOR ROOM ON THE LOWEST FLOOR OF A
STURDY BUILDING.
```

At 4:00 p.m., a tornado warning was issued that put Cordova in the polygon. The NWS in Birmingham described the tornado as "large and extremely dangerous," moving northeast at 55 mph.

The tornado that originated in Pickens County moved through the northwest corner of Tuscaloosa County and into southern Fayette County, where it moved over the small community of Boley Springs. Four people would lose their lives there; two couples, Leon and Sylvia Spruell, and Jeffery and Reba Kemp.

In Cordova, Julie, Malcolm, and Megan Johnson loaded up some supplies and headed for their storm cellar, about 20 yards away from the house. Julie's parents were neighbors, and they came over and got into the cellar as well, along with Julie's brother. In all, there were seven people and one dog in the small space. Megan said it was a tight fit, but as comfortable as could be under the circumstances.

They were glued to the live coverage on ABC 33/40 on that small battery-powered TV. They were paying very close attention to the words of Brian Peters and Tim Coleman who were in Walker County only about two miles southwest of them. As Brian and Tim described a large, multiple vortex tornado, Malcolm and his brother-in-law were outside at the entrance to the storm cellar. The sky was still blue, but debris began to fall from the sky ahead of the approaching tornado. Then, as the rain started to fall, the door to the storm cellar was shut, and within a minute it was on them.

Megan says in that small storm cellar it was loud, there was lots of suction, and ears were popping. Suddenly, it was much hotter. The tornado literally took the breath away from everyone. They knew hell on earth was being unleashed outside. To this day, Megan has a hard time going through a carwash. The noise at the end, when the jets begin to dry the car, reminds her of that horrible afternoon.

During the tornado, Malcolm and his brother-in-law both used all of their strength to keep the cellar door shut. The first thing to hit the door was their clothes dryer, followed by a small freezer.

Julie and the other family members thought this might be the end of their earthly journey despite the safety of the small space. There was fear the door would fail due to the large debris pounding the hillside, and setting up a likelihood that they would be literally sucked out and lofted by the tornado.

It took eight to ten seconds, but it felt like eight to ten minutes according to the family. When it stopped, Malcolm used all of his strength to open the storm cellar door; the dryer was lodged in front of it. His heart dropped when he looked toward their home to see that it was gone. Completely gone. All that was left was debris scattered on the hill above the cellar and across their property.

The storm cellar where 7 people on Riceton Road in Cordova survived the EF-4 tornado

The rest of the family worked their way out of the storm cellar, and at that moment they didn't know what to feel. Initially, they felt utter utter shock. Most wanted to cry, but they didn't even know what the tears were for just yet. After about 20 minutes, first responders were able to get through, finding all seven people safe and unharmed despite the devastation around them.

Darkness was coming quickly; and the Johnson family spent the night at Julie's parents' home, which wasn't touched by the tornado. The next day, it was time to start picking up the pieces. Hours and hours combing through rubble looking for anything meaningful that could be salvaged. The three family cats were found, and miraculously all of them survived. Ten days later, Megan noticed one of the cats walking in an odd way. After taking the cat to the veterinarian, the vet removed two three-inch pieces of a mirror that were pulled out of the cat's hip. You have to wonder what that cat was thinking during the tornado. Animals have a strong survival instinct.

The Johnson family knows they were very fortunate on April 27, 2011, despite losing their home. The evening tornado killed four people in Cordova, including Jackson Van Horn, the son of Megan's bus driver. The Van Horn family was huddled together in their basement when part of the house collapsed on them.

Brothers Jonathan Doss, 12, and Justin Doss, 10, were killed while taking refuge from the storm in the home of Annette Singleton, who also lost her life. The Doss brothers had been throwing a football in a local park with Annette's son, 16-year-old Madison Phillips, before the afternoon storm. Madison survived, although he suffered a significant head injury.

After passing through Cordova, the EF-4 tornado clipped the southern tip of Cullman County before moving into Blount County. It finally lifted in Marshall County, and the path length was 128 miles.

Downtown Cordova after the two tornadoes of
April 27, 2011. Photo from Crystal Kilgore.

In the days following the tornado, a community relief effort was built at the high school and supported by local churches. It was a well-oiled machine. They matched the "needs" with the "haves" for days before any federal or state officials showed up. People from different parts of Alabama and the U.S. sent supplies that were urgently needed. The distribution process was efficient and effective.

Megan Johnson says they didn't lose their lives because "God wasn't finished with us yet". She shared her story with me because she believes when more tornado stories like theirs are told, more people will take warnings seriously. It doesn't always happen to someone else. You aren't protected from a tornado due to a ridge, valley, body of water, or words your grandparents say.

If you pay attention to the weather, have a good way of hearing warnings, and have a plan on getting to a safe place, you have a greater chance of survival, just like the Johnson family. Even during a violent EF-4.

A couple of weeks after the tornado, Megan was looking at a Facebook page set up for people who found photos and other items lofted from the 62 Alabama tornadoes. She was shocked to see Malcolm and Julie's wedding photo on the site; it was found in Flat Rock, Alabama, 109 miles to the northeast. They contacted the person who found it, and in turn, the person mailed the print back to the Johnsons along with a gift card. The frame was gone, but the print made the journey crumpled, but intact.

Malcolm and Julie Johnson's wedding photo carried over 100 miles by the Cordova tornado on April 27, 2011.

The Johnsons built back on the same lot on Riceton Road in Cordova a year after the tornado. And, they now have a new, larger storm cellar, with better access.

The Johnson's home on Riceton Road before the tornado (top), the destroyed home the day after the tornado (middle), and their current home (bottom) on the same property.

Cordova's only grocery store, Piggly Wiggly, celebrated its grand re-opening in November 2014. The City of Cordova built a new City Hall and police and fire station which opened in the summer of 2015. Much of downtown Cordova remains vacant today, but the people have their spirit back and believe the future is bright for the Walker County town.

A memorial recognizing Jonathan and Justin Doss, Jackson Van Horn, and Annette Singleton has been erected, a marker that will remind future generations of that horrible day in April of 2011 when two tornadoes tore through the same small town.

CHAPTER 14: HOSPITAL HEROES

My first experience with DCH Regional Medical Center came in 1968 when at the age of 12 I had a bone tumor removed from the middle finger on my right hand. Dr. E.C. Brock performed the surgery; the tumor thankfully was benign. Many remember Dr. Brock from his years of service as team doctor for the University of Alabama football team from 1959 to 1982, mostly during the tenure of Coach Paul "Bear" Bryant. DCH in those days was simply "Druid City Hospital". I am thankful for the care I received there as a child, and many more are thankful for the services performed by that same medical facility on April 27, 2011.

I dipped my toe into healthcare in 2005 when I accepted the role of Chairman of the Board of Trustees of a large hospital in Birmingham. What was to be a two-year hitch has grown to 16 years as of this writing, and I still have much to learn. Healthcare is a challenging business full of amazing people, including both clinical and non-clinical workers. These workers are people with hearts for serving others with their powerful platform.

I have always been intrigued by the emergency department. These professionals come to work on a daily basis with no idea of what to expect on their shifts. There is tremendous variety in patient acuity, volume, and stress levels. But like other departments in a hospital, most who work there feel a calling. They are uniquely qualified to handle a wide variety of situations, from a broken toe to severe, life-threatening trauma.

In the hospital business, the term "mass casualty" refers to a combination of patient numbers and care requirements that challenge or exceed the hospital's ability to provide adequate patient care using day-to-day operations.

All hospitals must be prepared to provide rapid triage and treatment to large numbers of patients after disasters. At DCH, they have plans in place for unidentified patients during an MCI (Mass Casualty Incident) to temporarily track them without names or other identifying information. Their plan involves hundreds of trauma packets with bar-coded armbands set up with generic names for patient tracking purposes.

Most hospitals conduct table-top exercises regularly involving key personnel discussing MCI scenarios in an informal setting. In 2010, a group from Tuscaloosa, including some from DCH, went to the National Fire Academy in Emmitsburg, Maryland, for a five-day training course. The simulated disaster project worked on by the group just happened to be a tornado. Those from Tuscaloosa involved in that training in Maryland had no idea this disaster preparation would be put into use less than six months later.

Those in administration at DCH, as well as those in the Emergency Department, were aware of the severe weather threat coming in late April 2011. Like football coaches, farmers, and those in construction, those who work in a hospital tend to keep a close eye on the weather, especially when it becomes threatening.

Terri Snider, Nurse Manager in the DCH Emergency Department at the time of the generational tornado event, says they were staffed for a normal operational day on April 27, 2011, but had many staff members on standby in case they were needed.

The early morning EF-3 tornado that moved through the eastern part of Tuscaloosa County, east of the City of Tuscaloosa, tore through the community of Coaling a little before 5:30 a.m. Eight people were transported to DCH, including five from the same family. Only one of the family required admittance as a patient.

Dr. Elwin Crawford, who was on duty that morning (and stayed through the evening event), says the one seriously injured patient came in with one shoe off and one shoe on; that patient said the tornado "blew his shoe off" while destroying their home in Coaling. The patient was treated for three broken ribs and a collapsed lung, injuries he sustained when he was hit by a flying appliance during the tornado.

The middle of the day April 27, 2011, was fairly routine in the Emergency Department. Staff nurse Sharon Oakley said everyone on duty had a strange feeling, that however, knowing "something would happen". An incident command center was set up in administration; the weather was being constantly monitored throughout the day by CEO Bryan Kindred and other members of his team.

The City of Tuscaloosa went into the polygon at 4:47 p.m.

```
BULLETIN - EAS ACTIVATION REQUESTED
TORNADO WARNING
NATIONAL WEATHER SERVICE BIRMINGHAM AL
447 PM CDT WED APR 27 2011

THE NATIONAL WEATHER SERVICE IN BIRMINGHAM HAS ISSUED A

* TORNADO WARNING FOR...
  NORTHEASTERN GREENE COUNTY IN WEST CENTRAL ALABAMA...
  SOUTHEASTERN PICKENS COUNTY IN WEST CENTRAL ALABAMA...
  TUSCALOOSA COUNTY IN WEST CENTRAL ALABAMA...

* UNTIL 545 PM CDT

* AT 443 PM CDT...THE NATIONAL WEATHER SERVICE INDICATED A SEVERE
  THUNDERSTORM CAPABLE OF PRODUCING A TORNADO. THIS DANGEROUS STORM
  WAS LOCATED NEAR MANTUA...OR 14 MILES NORTH OF EUTAW...AND MOVING
  NORTHEAST AT 55 MPH.

* LOCATIONS IMPACTED INCLUDE...
  NORTHPORT...TUSCALOOSA...HOLT...JENA...COKER...LAKE LURLEEN STATE
  PARK...BRYANT DENNY STADIUM...MCFARLAND MALL...UNIVERSITY MALL AND
  DEERLICK CREEK CAMPGROUNDS.

THIS INCLUDES...
INTERSTATE 20 EXIT NUMBERS 52 THROUGH 97...

PRECAUTIONARY/PREPAREDNESS ACTIONS...

TAKE COVER NOW. FOR YOUR PROTECTION MOVE TO AN INTERIOR ROOM ON THE
LOWEST FLOOR OF A STURDY BUILDING.
```

**The tornado warning issued for Tuscaloosa
County at 4:47 p.m. on April 27, 2011**

Right away, people in the Emergency Department waiting room were moved down to an auditorium that offered better protection. Any patients who could be moved were taken upstairs to free up space in the Emergency Department, in case a tornado did touch down. Sharon Oakley was part of a team caring for a 3-year-old seizure patient in the trauma hall. The little girl was intubated, and couldn't be moved; Oakley and another nurse on the unit, Sharon Allen, huddled over her for protection as the tornado approached.

Other staff members, watching our live coverage, grew increasingly concerned as it seemed as though the tornado was moving right toward them. Most got under desks or into small interior spaces, bracing for a potential hit. Elsewhere in the hospital patients were taken into interior hallways, away from windows.

Candi Hagler was nurse manager on 6th Floor North on April 27, 2011. On the south end of that floor there is a huge window that faces southwest, toward 15th Street. That gave them a spectacular, but at the same time horrifying view of the tornado. Candi says there "was a lot of praying" going on" after the hospital tornado safety plan was implemented. Patients, family members, nurses, and other hospital employees asked God to spare them and the facility. It is her belief that those powerful prayers were heard.

Security cameras showed the tornado getting closer, and fire alarms in the building started to sound. Ears were popping due to the pressure change. There was a very loud roar.

The Tuscaloosa EF-4 tornado, captured by a security camera at DCH Regional Medical Center as it passed just south of the hospital.

Less than a minute later, the roar stopped, and the staff breathed a sigh of relief knowing the building was intact. Dr. Crawford, who went to the incident command center, came in immediately to let everyone know that damage reports were coming in fast and furious, and they needed to get ready for a very long night.

The EF-4 tornado, almost miraculously, cut a path between University Mall and DCH. The core passed only one-quarter mile south of the hospital. There was no structural damage to the building, but commercial power was lost and water pressure dropped severely. The facility quickly came back up on generator power.

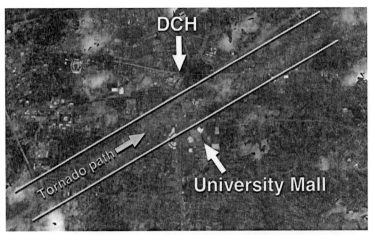

On May 2, 2011, the Advanced Land Imager (ALI) on NASA's Earth Observing-1 (EO-1) satellite captured this natural-color image of the tornado track through Tuscaloosa.

The first 15 to 20 minutes after the tornado were eerily quiet. The first call to Dr. Crawford was from Tuscaloosa Fire and Rescue from 10th Avenue, in front of Rosedale Court with a 188-unit public housing project. Paramedics had three infants, all in cardiac arrest.

In an MCI, typically you don't bring those patients to a hospital; they are pronounced dead on the scene. But a paramedic told Dr. Crawford the parents brought the infants to them in their arms, begging for help. He had to do something, and the decision was made to transport them. The three infants were the first to arrive at DCH. The paramedic in the back of that ambulance did everything he could, but they were pronounced deceased as soon as they were taken out of the ambulance. It was heartbreaking, but there was no time to grieve.

Terri Snider says people were coming in the front door of the E.D. "in droves". She says the first severely injured person she can recall was brought to the hospital in the back of a pick-up truck, and was carried into the triage area on a piece of plywood. A young woman with him was treated but didn't survive.

People kept pouring in the front door. They were on countertops, doors, parts of beds, or anything else that would act as a stretcher. The scene was controlled chaos. In the hospital, many who were hurt opted to wait for medical help knowing there were others with life-threatening injuries. Frantic people were looking for missing friends or relatives. Kids without parents, and parents without kids. Even dogs and cats were seen running down the hallways.

While the initial surge of patients was brought in via private vehicles, a steady flow of rescue vehicles followed. In some cases, one ambulance would be transporting anywhere from two to four patients.

Some of the injured who were ambulatory walked to the hospital from places like Alberta City. Some were bleeding, some in shock. They were just walking toward that light on a hill, in the direction of the "helpers" that Fred Rogers told children about on his long-running television show, Mr. Rogers Neighborhood.

"When I was a boy and I would see scary things in the news, my mother would say to me, "Look for the helpers. You will always find people who are helping." To this day, especially in times of "disaster," I remember my mother's words, and I am always comforted by realizing that there

are still so many helpers – so many caring people in this world."

Off-duty nurses and doctors streamed into the hospital; nobody had to be called in. The medical professionals at DCH Regional Medical Center that night were ready and focused, but dealing with so much - severed limbs, amputations, impaled objects, fractures, death. In triage, clinicians were having to discern which patients to treat first based on their likelihood of surviving.

All hospital employees played a role that night, even those in dietary services, housekeeping, and maintenance. All stepped up to the plate with empathy, performing services way beyond their normal duties.

Dr. Crawford said the E.D. volume was overwhelming for the staff during the first thirty minutes, but once other physicians arrived, they could "breathe a bit".

Some seriously injured patients needing surgery had to be transferred to other hospitals in the Birmingham area because of the water pressure issue; instruments couldn't be sterilized. The Cedar Crest neighborhood, just southwest of the hospital, was pretty much wiped out, and water lines were broken, disrupting service to DCH.

According to Terri Snider, one of the most amazing things about the night was how people were so patient. Often care was turned down by people in the E.D. who told nurses and physicians to find others who were more seriously injured. Patients, despite their injuries, were asking the clinicians how they could help. Terri says it was a "blessing out of a disaster" to see this kind of compassion.

The DCH parking deck was a hodgepodge of activity; some from the community drove into the lower levels using it as a shelter before the tornado, and they wound up staying there because roads were blocked and there was no way back to their homes. A few families spent the night in the parking deck. Some were seen with portable grills and sleeping bags.

Brenda Henry was working at DCH on April 27, 2011 as a surgical nurse on the second floor. As she watched the approach of the tornado on a monitor, she "made peace with God" during the moment. She wondered if she'd spent enough time with her kids. She wondered if she was ready for her final day on Earth. For those few seconds, it was a time of prayer and reflection as a monster tornado approached.

Then, it was time to get focused. Brenda made sure the trauma room was ready and every room had a flashlight. As the tornado passed, she was thinking about how many would be coming in, knowing things were about to ramp up quickly. It was her "narrow-focus" mode.

Trauma cases were nothing new for Brenda, but the first patient under her watch was a young woman who was covered in dirt. The process of washing that dirt off of her body, and seeing the serious nature of her injuries, was almost overwhelming. She was young, and someone's child. Brenda was still not lost in emotion, but laser-focused on her care. She told me the young woman had the "best of the best" working on her April 27, 2011. The anesthesia crew, five surgeons, and surgical technicians.

According to Brenda Henry, the young woman "fought harder than anyone else I have ever seen in a trauma situation". That woman went into cardiac arrest on a stretcher after surgery, on the way to an ICU room. Despite a very prolonged effort to bring her back, she died at DCH Regional Medical Center that night.

Brenda had to transport the young woman to the hospital morgue with others who were killed by the tornado. After this, she had to have a break for a few minutes and walked to the front of the hospital on level one, where she saw people lined up trying to get into the emergency room. There was simply nowhere to go for a break, so she went back to the second floor to work other cases. It was a night that seemed as if it would never end.

Hospital records show that 600 were treated in the Emergency Department, but those were only the patients who were registered. Less acute patients went to other centers set up in the hospital building, not going through the E.D. It is estimated that around 1,000 patients were treated the night of April 27, 2011.

**Tuscaloosa's DCH Regional Medical Center
after the April 27, 2011, EF-4 tornado.
Photo from Jimmy Warren/Totalcom Marketing.**

Many lessons were learned that night by those at DCH. All told me, "take it seriously". Tornadoes impact real people, at a real place, and in real-time. With their own eyes, they saw human suffering and loss of life. It doesn't always happen to "someone else" in "another part of town".

Ron Howard, Director of Pastoral Care Services at DCH, told me, "I still see the faces of the four dead children that were placed in my care and of the days it took to find their families. I served 26 years as a Navy Chaplain including a tour as Command Chaplain at Bethesda National Naval Medical Center at the height of the

Iraq/Afghanistan Wars dealing with all of the combat head injuries. Nothing compares to that evening of April 27th. The work of the DCH staff was incredible but, unfortunately, has had lasting effects."

He penned "A Caregivers Prayer" in the days following April 27, 2011. This is posted in the hospital today adjacent to the room where the incident command center was set up the day of the tornado.

A CAREGIVERS PRAYER

In the midst of disaster,
Lord, as caregivers, we find ourselves still in shock
By what nature's fury has wrought.
We are overcome by the amount of devastation
And how close the destruction came to our hospital.
We find ourselves becoming disoriented
As we travel around our community.
Our familiar landmarks are gone.
And we feel lost in our own city.
Yet we stand in Rosedale and look down the path of destruction,
We see something previously we could not.
DCH standing on the hill.
When we are disoriented in Forest Lake. We look around and
We see DCH standing on the hill.
When we are wiping tears from our eyes in Alberta City,
We see DCH standing on the hill.
After the tornado passed, our community saw DCH standing here.
And, by the hundreds they came -
The wounded, the dying, the homeless, the scared.

They came because they knew that we could not
hide our light.
That the skill of our staff would brightly shine.
That we could care for them with compassion and skill.
We give thanks for our employees, physicians, and
volunteers,
Who worked tirelessly to meet our community's needs
At our hospitals and in the community.
We pray for comfort for the families who are grieving, and
For families that have suffered loss.
Lord, most of all, we pray for healing.
Amen.

CHAPTER 15: RIDING OUT AN
EF-5 IN A BATHTUB

The most violent tornadoes are also the rarest. The Enhanced Fujita (EF) tornado scale rates the intensity of tornadoes based on the damage they produce. The scale runs from zero to five; most tornadoes are at the lower end of the scale, EF-0 and EF-1 strength.

EF-4 and EF-5 tornadoes represent only about two percent of all tornadoes recorded in the U.S. Since 1950 nationally, there have been only 59 EF-5 tornadoes (based on data from the Storm Prediction Center); seven of those in Alabama.

By definition, an EF-5 tornado has winds of 200 mph or greater and creates "incredible damage." Well-built frame houses are destroyed with foundations swept clean of debris; steel-reinforced concrete structures are critically damaged; tall buildings collapse or have severe structural deformations; cars, trucks, and trains can be thrown approximately 1 mile".

Three EF-5s touched down in our state during the April 3-4, 1974 Superoutbreak. The next EF-5 came 24 years later, on April 8, 1998 in the western part of the Birmingham metro area. The other three came on April 27, 2011.

Two of those three moved through Marion County, in the northwest part of the state. One of those had been down in Northeast Mississippi, producing catastrophic damage in the town of Smithville before moving into Alabama. The other one moved through Hackleburg and Phil Campbell, then across parts of the Tennessee Valley.

I can honestly say the two most violent tornadoes in Alabama in my lifetime were the Guin EF-5 on April 3, 1974, and the Hackleburg/Phil Campbell tornado in 2011. I saw the damage with my own eyes, and it is simply indescribable. Any tree left standing was debarked, and in some cases, the ground was scoured.

The third EF-5 on April 27, 2011 came in DeKalb County, in Northeast Alabama. The tornado touched down near the Lakeview community, then moved northeastward near Fyffe, Rainsville, Sylvania, Henegar, Ider, and eventually into northern DeKalb County south of the Cartersville community.

Lacey Edgeworth, along with her husband Jeremy, and 18-month-old son Cooper, lived in rural DeKalb County in 2011, east of the community of Henegar on Alabama Highway 117.

Monday and Tuesday, April 25-26, were routine days for Lacy, a busy mom. She woke up, cooked, cleaned, changed Cooper's diapers, took him outside to play, bathed him and got him in bed.

Monday night while she was taking a shower, she felt the need to pray. Lacey says she asked God to protect her and her family if they ever had to be in that bathtub during a storm. Little did she know He would answer that prayer in just 48 hours.

On Wednesday morning, April 27, a morning thunderstorm had produced some scattered damage in the area, and power was out at the Edgeworths' home. At that time in her life, Lacey says, "storms meant nothing to me", and there was no concern about the weather. But, at the same time, Lacey told me, "in my heart, I knew something was wrong; I just didn't know what it was".

Jeremy went to work as usual, but a few hours later Jeremy called to let Lacey know he was being sent home due to the high risk of severe thunderstorms and tornadoes. Lacey let Cooper play outside during a few passing afternoon showers, but the weather was still fairly benign, although windy.

Around 5:30 Lacey took Cooper in to dry him off and got him into his pajamas. About an hour later, Lacey decided to change clothes in case severe storms did strike and she had to get out and help people. She noticed her clothes didn't match and she knew if she got caught outside not matching her mom would kill her. After getting the clothes coordinated, she started to light candles and get ready for nighttime.

Around 6:40, Jeremy got a call from "Code Red", a severe weather warning service offered by the DeKalb County Emergency Management Agency. After the call, he went to look out the utility room window and saw the approaching storm.

Fuzzy flip-phone image of the EF-5 tornado at Sylvania, about 10 miles southwest of the Edgeworths' home. Photo from Bobby Abbott.

Jeremy yelled at Lacey to get Cooper and get into the bathroom. The house was getting dark and they couldn't find Cooper. Finally they saw him in a corner playing with their corded phone. As they headed to the bathroom Lacey grabbed the pillows off their bed, not really thinking that they even needed them. Jeremy then looked out the bathroom window and saw a huge, gray tornado headed their way.

They got down in the tub and started to pray, "please Lord protect us, please Lord protect us". Cooper was screaming because he didn't understand why Lacey was holding him down in the tub under pillows. As Lacey and Jeremy continued to cry out to God, they could hear the tornado ripping their house to pieces about twenty seconds after getting in the bathtub. Lacey was screaming, "Jesus, Jesus, Jesus protect us."

Lacey told me, "I knew I was taking my last few breaths of life." She says she was at peace with dying at that moment. The tornado lofted them, throwing them up and out of the house while still in the tub, which was a full bath/shower combo. With nothing covering their heads, they felt helpless. And, they couldn't breathe because of the insulation and debris. All Lacey could do was stare at Cooper's face to make sure he was breathing. Lacey could hear Jeremy saying, "just hold on. Just keep holding on".

After coming back down to the ground, the only part of the bath/shower combo remaining was under them, and they were surrounded by trees and wood from the walls of their home which formed a type of shelter. That shelter protected the family of three from the debris and shrapnel in the tornado until the wind finally stopped.

**The Edgeworth family survived the
tornado in this bathtub.**

After the tornado, Lacey could hear Jeremy, but couldn't
see him. But she was comforted for her knowing he was
alive. Cooper was still in her arms and was breathing
after she dug dirt out of his mouth. The family dog
appeared from who knows where.

**All that was left of the Edgeworth's home
after the April 27, 2011 tornado.**

Lacey had two cuts, one on her ankle and one on her wrist. Cooper had a small knot on his forehead. Jeremy was uninjured.

A total of 35 people lost their lives in DeKalb County that night; the Edgeworth family was spared. Very few people on the planet can say they survived an EF-5 tornado, but Lacey, Jeremy, and Cooper did, in their words, "by the grace of God". They opted to rebuild on the same property; their house today sits on the exact same spot on Highway 117.

Jeremy, Cooper, and Lacey Edgeworth after the April 27, 2011 tornado that destroyed their home.

During the day April 27, 2011, Lacey told me she took "picture after picture". For this book she sent me one picture of her and Cooper. She said, "it is terrible, and after I took it I thought I would hate for this to be my last picture, so I almost hit the delete button. But for some reason I couldn't delete it. If we had not made it through the storm that would have been the last picture of me."

The photograph Lacey Edgeworth took that was almost deleted on April 27, 2011, just hours before their home was destroyed.

Thankfully, the Edgeworth family did make it through the storm. They survived an EF-5 tornado in a bathtub, by God's grace.

CHAPTER 16: FIVE CASKETS, ONE FAMILY

The EF-4 tornado that moved through Cullman was well documented. We had it live on our SKYCAM on ABC 33/40 as it tore through the city. But the story didn't end at Cullman. The twister stayed on the ground another 30 miles, through the southeast tip of Morgan County, and into Marshall County, finally lifting near the Tennessee River.

Six-year-old Ari Hallmark was a kindergarten student at Brindlee Mountain Primary School, but school was canceled on April 27, 2011, due to the severe weather situation. She spent part of the day with her dad, Shane, who was doing work on the family chicken farm in Union Grove. There was debris to be cleaned up from the morning round of storms. Trees were down and needed to be cleared.

Ari's mom, Jennifer, was in nursing school at Snead State Community College. An important final exam was scheduled for the day, and Jennifer went on to the school that morning in Boaz with her sister-in-law, Mandy Garmany, who was also in nursing school. Jennifer got back around noon and picked up Ari; from there they went to their new house in the Ruth community, just northwest of Arab. They had been living there for only about ten days.

Shane, Jennifer, and Ari Hallmark

Ari and her mom were aware of the severe weather threat and were paying attention to weather updates during the afternoon as they were doing chores in the new house. Shane came home from the farm during the afternoon and the family discussed the pending storms. Shane didn't believe it would be that bad at their home;

after all, severe storms usually happened somewhere else. Not there.

But Shane saw what was happening in Cullman and knew it would be a very rough ride. The family planned on going to Shane's parents' house, just a few minutes away by car, to pick up his mom and dad, Ann and Phillip, and 17-month-old twins that they were babysitting. The toddlers, Jayden and Julie, were the children of Ricky and Regina Hallmark; Ricky is Shane's brother.

Jayden and Julie Hallmark

Regina worked at Alfa Insurance in Huntsville and Ricky worked at Golden Living Center in Arab. Regina was asked to help out in Arab because the office was covered up with claims due to the morning round of storms.

The plan was to get Ann, Phillip, and the twins back to Shane and Jennifer's new home so they could ride out the storm together there. Ari just wanted her dad to pick them up so she and Jennifer could stay home, but the decision was made for all three to make the short trip together. Ari told me she knew something bad was going to happen soon because of a series of dreams in recent months. She didn't know it would be an EF-4 tornado.

Phillip and Ann Hallmark

Minutes after Ari, Shane, and Jennifer walked into Ann and Phillip's home, the power went out, and everyone could see a large, violent tornado only about 100 yards away churning toward them. There was no time to go back, they would have to ride it out right there.

Two others were there, family member Jordin Putnum and friend Harold Buchanan. In all, there were nine souls in that home.

They all crammed into a small bathroom near the center of the house. Ann Hallmark did her best to reassure everyone, telling them that it was going to be okay. Ari remembers her dad trying to prevent the door and walls from collapsing, then grabbing her and holding tightly. Later, it was determined that Ari had severely bruised ribs because Shane was holding her so tight, protecting her and probably saving her life.

The EF-4 tornado crossing U.S. 231 after moving through the Ruth community on April 27, 2011. Photo by Charles Whisenant, The Arab Tribune

Ari's next memory was waking up in a field; she immediately began to cry out for her parents. She tried to open her eyes, but she couldn't see anything because of dirt and blood. Then, she blacked out again. She has no recollection of being found in that field 200 yards away from her grandparents' home by a neighbor, Kenny Casey. He carried the girl in his arms almost a mile to Ruth Road before meeting emergency workers.

Ari was transported to Marshall Medical Center North in Guntersville, and after being stabilized she was moved to the trauma center at Huntsville Hospital. Ari had a fractured skull and a broken collarbone and left arm, with multiple severe cuts and lacerations. Her wounds required 18 staples and 66 stitches. But she was alive.

One of the toddler twins, Julie, was found alive and transported with Ari. Julie's brain had a small bleed, and she had severe head trauma and a lacerated liver. Both lungs had collapsed, and she had a broken collarbone and left arm with multiple cuts and lacerations. At Huntsville, Julie underwent surgery to put drains in her lungs.

This is where five members of the Hallmark family were killed April 27, 2011 in the Ruth community. Photo by Charles Whisenant, The Arab Tribune

The other twin, Jayden, didn't survive the tornado. Also killed were Shane, Jennifer, Ann, and Phillip -- Ari's parents, maternal grandparents, and cousin. Five of the nine in the house died; Jordin Putnum and Harold Buchanan survived.

Every seat was filled for the joint funeral at Union Hill First Congregational Methodist Church. Five caskets, all with red roses, except Jayden's, which had white roses. One family. Ari didn't attend the funeral based on her wishes and advice from surviving family members. But she did come to the visitation, which was enough for her. Very few, especially at the age of six, attend a five-casket visitation. Ari's kindergarten teacher stayed with her during the funeral so all of the family members could attend.

The month following the tornado, Ari walked on stage at Snead State Community College's graduation of nursing students and received her mother's Florence Nightingale pin. Jennifer was the valedictorian of her nursing class; Ari stood in her mom's place during graduation, alongside her aunt Mandy Garmany.

Ari, now 16, says she deals with the family tragedy these days by talking about it to others. Especially others her age who have lost their parents. She says for the first few years after the tornado, she was terrified of storms. But now she has accepted the results of April 27, 2011 as God's will, and her PTSD has faded.

In 2019, Ari Hallmark was crowned the 2019 Arab Junior High Sweetheart. At AJHS Ari was a cheerleader and a member of the Beta Club. She lives in Ruth with her maternal grandmother, Susan Garmany. They are in the same home that Ari, Shane, and Jennifer moved into, newly built, ten days before the April 27, 2011 tornado.

Ironically, it wasn't touched, while Ann and Phillip Hallmark's house was destroyed just a short distance away.

After Ari lost consciousness as she was being lifted by the tornado in 2011, she became aware of a long, white staircase. Then, there was a large group of people walking up those stairs. And with the group, there was a being Ari describes as an angel, who was leading the way to a place some call heaven.

The journey up the stairs was long, but there was no fatigue. Ari then, during those moments in time, saw her grandfather, who had died several years ago, along with her parents, Shane and Jennifer, her grandparents, Phillip and Ann, and her cousin Jayden. Ari says they all looked strong and healthy. Shane had a condition called Alopecia that left him with no facial hair, eyebrows, eyelashes, or any hair on his head, but in heaven Shane had a full head of hair. On Earth, Shane was almost legally blind, but this time there were no glasses. After getting to see her family, she was told it was time to go back down the stairs, and soon after that she remembered crying in that field in Marshall County, Alabama.

The year after the tornado at the age of 7, Ari, with help from Lisa Reburn, wrote a book about her near-death experience called "To Heaven After the Storm". The proceeds from Ari's book are helping a ministry for other children dealing with death. I hope you consider getting a copy; the e-book version is available on almost every platform. It is a remarkable and encouraging read.

**Ari Hallmark showing off her book,
"To Heaven After the Storm"**

As she entered her teenage years, Ari says she went
through several phases about the question "Why?" Why
were my family members taken? Why in the world did this
happen in the first place?

Ari became angry at God, at her friends, at life in general.
When this happened, Susan Garmany, Ari's grandmother
encouraged her to go work with Thursday's Child, a
ministry that helps disabled children and their parents.
After working with this group, Ari says she realized just
how lucky and blessed she was just to be alive.

Her mission now is to encourage others, share God's love, and let them know heaven is a real place.

From time to time, Ari and Susan make the one and-a-half mile drive from their home to the spot where five family members perished in the April 27, 2011 tornado. Painful memories, but comforting knowing they will be reunited at another place at another time.

Ari says she has two main career choices now, becoming a PICU (Pediatric Intensive Care Unit) nurse or a meteorologist. I can tell you now she will be successful at either one she chooses.

In all, there were 15 tornadoes in Marshall County alone on April 27, 2011, including the EF-4 responsible for the deaths of the five members of the Hallmark family. A total of 47 people were injured, and the damage was estimated at 30 million dollars in the county.

CHAPTER 17: RASCAL
THE TORNADO CAT

In April 2011 Laura Ogden lived in Concord with her husband George, along with their dog Gizmo and cat Rascal. Laura was at work on April 27; her older sister kept calling, telling her she needed to go home because of the tornado threat. Finally, she relented and went home. Laura told me one hour later, she didn't have a home.

When the EF-4 tornado came through, Laura was home with George and some neighbors who came over because Laura's house had a basement. They all noticed debris falling from the sky, and everyone went to the basement. Laura told me that within seconds the "house exploded" above them as the tornado passed through. George had some broken ribs and the entire group went to Bessemer Carraway Hospital.

The home of George and Laura Ogden on Smith Road in Concord after the EF-4 tornado.
Photo from Laura Ogden.

George was released and the next morning he went back to their home property to see what was left. While they were looking at the damage, their dog, Gizmo, came walking up to the house with some neighbors. The dog was still covered in debris but was fine.

But the search for the cat, Rascal, was unsuccessful. George and Laura concluded that Rascal died in the tornado. A "tornado replacement cat" they named Sylvester showed up a day or two after the storm, and would wind up living with the Ogdens. They have no idea where Sylvester came from, but they knew he chose them for some reason.

The Ogdens' son, Daniel, and his friends worked for days on the property salvaging personal belongings. Photo from Laura Ogden.

Their insurance company brought a camper to the property, and George, Laura, Gizmo, and Sylvester lived there while their home was being rebuilt. On July 11, 75 days after the tornado, Laura kept hearing a cat. She went outside with George and they saw the cat under a truck on the property. Looking closely, with almost disbelief, they realized their long-lost cat Rascal... the one they thought was killed in the tornado.

George said, "He wasn't anything but a bag of bones," but Rascal was home. However, he was far from being in perfect condition. His collar had somehow managed to get tangled up in his front left leg. The Ogdens took Rascal to veterinarian David Langford, who said the cat was on the verge of cutting his leg off. The eleven-pound cat was only two pounds when he came home after his unknown journey following the tornado.

Dr. Langford performed surgery by cutting off bad tissue, piecing muscle back together and repairing skin. The aftermath... about 30 staples. Laura and George took Rascal home, but Rascal tore his leg open again, meaning another trip to the vet. After multiple days, Rascal's condition went downhill, and Langford called the Ogdens to tell them he was going to have to put Rascal down to keep him out of pain and misery.

The Ogdens gave him permission, but the next morning they got a call from Dr. Langford, who said he just couldn't do it. About two weeks later, Rascal had a heart attack and passed away.

Laura Ogden has no idea where Rascal was for those 75 days after the tornado, but was impressed he knew the way back home, since there was no home left. All of her photos of Rascal were destroyed in the tornado, but memories of "Rascal the tornado cat" will live on in their hearts and minds.

CHAPTER 18: SURVIVAL ON A BOAT

The EF-4 tornado that tore through Tuscaloosa and the western part of Birmingham on April 27, 2011, got lots of attention since it moved through two population centers in Alabama and impacted so many people. This tornado was produced by a supercell thunderstorm that began in Newton County, Mississippi, at 2:54 p.m. CT, and finally dissipated in Macon County, North Carolina, at approximately 10:18 p.m. CT. This supercell existed for 7 hours and 24 minutes, and traveled approximately 380 miles producing several strong to violent tornadoes along the way.

One particular tornado first touched down in Greene County, north of Eutaw, and lifted just north of downtown Birmingham. It was down for 81 miles, and at one point was a mile and a half wide (crossing I-65 north of downtown Birmingham). Maximum winds were 190 mph, and it was responsible for the deaths of 65 people, along with approximately 1,500 injuries.

Media covered the destruction in Tuscaloosa and Birmingham extensively. But what about that area between the two cities? Their story isn't known by most people since there was so little coverage of the damage in rural parts of eastern Tuscaloosa and western Jefferson counties. Not faulting journalists here; they were overwhelmed with so many tornado stories to cover.

I do see this over and over, however; local TV stations providing "wall to wall" severe weather coverage when tornadoes are threatening a metropolitan area, then simply going back to regular programming when the storms, still dangerous and life threatening, move into sparsely populated areas. That makes absolutely no sense. Lives are precious in the city and away from the city.

In 2011, Ed and Shirley Cook lived on Recreation Area Road in Peterson, a small community northeast of Tuscaloosa. Their mobile home is within walking distance of the Black Warrior River, where their boat is docked at Hide-A-Way Harbor Marina. For many years they would travel down the river through the Holt Lock and Dam to Manderson Landing, along Jack Warner Parkway in Tuscaloosa, when Alabama had a home football game.

On April 27, the Cooks were sitting on their porch that afternoon, noting the weather was windy and warm. Knowing severe storms were coming, Ed suggested that Shirley take the short drive down to their boat at the marina, believing the 28-foot cruiser would be safer than their mobile home. After watching severe weather coverage on TV, Ed joined Shirley later, and their decision turned out to be a good one.

Soon after Ed got on the boat with Shirley, the tornado was ripping a path through the heart of Tuscaloosa, and the community of Holt. The wind in the tornado at Holt was estimated at 190 mph by the National Weather Service team that surveyed the damage.

I drive through that area often; I use the Brookwood-Holt backroads as a path to Bryant-Denny Stadium on Saturdays in the fall when I provide weather support to the University of Alabama athletic department during home football games. To this day, it takes my breath away when I cross the tornado path. I seriously wonder if it actually reached EF-5 strength as it moved over Hurricane Creek.

The tornado tore apart a large metal railroad trestle with a 500-foot span over the creek, and a metal truss support structure weighing 75,000 pounds was thrown 100 feet up on a nearby hill. I wish that part of the path could be evaluated again; I am no structural engineer, but I have gone on many tornado damage surveys over the years, and I firmly believe this was EF-5 damage. One criterion for rating an EF-5 is "steel-reinforced concrete structures are critically damaged." Part of this well-built bridge was blown away.

The railroad trestle over Hurricane Creek destroyed by the April 27, 2011 tornado. Photo from Bill Castle/ABC 33/40

From the back of their boat (only about two miles northeast of the Hurricane Creek bridge that was destroyed), they witnessed the large tornado approaching from the southwest with "debris flying everywhere". Shirley told me she went down the stairs into the lower part of the boat and prayed, thinking they were about to die. Ed stayed on the deck and watched.

The wind tipped the boat over to about a 12-degree angle, Ed tells me, and his ears were ringing from the noise. As it turns out, the tornado passed just south of the marina where their boat was docked. Their lives were spared, but the tornado moved directly over their property, destroying the mobile home and most of their belongings.

Ed and Shirley Cook survived the tornado on their boat, only a quarter of a mile northwest of their home, which was destroyed.

After the tornado's passage, Ed and Shirley immediately left the boat to check on their home, but the road was blocked by fallen trees. Ed and some other men from the marina jumped over the trees, made their way up the hill to Recreation Area Road. There, they were able to get chainsaws from neighbors, clearing a path for others at the marina. When Shirley made it through the debris to their property, the scene was heartbreaking. "There was nothing left. Nothing," she told me. "The whole neighborhood was gone; it looked like a bomb went off."

Shirley told me she saw some of her possessions across the road, including a shower curtain wrapped around the one lone tree still standing. Later she found her washer and dryer down the hill, toward the river, with some dirty clothes still "hanging out of the washer."

**The Cook property in Peterson after the tornado.
Photo from Jake Cook.**

A nearby tornado siren was toppled. A clock was found that stopped at 5:17 p.m.

Most of the Cooks' neighbors survived. About 20 people took shelter in a large drainage pipe.

However, one of the neighbors, Graham Davie, was killed by the tornado. Davie's body was found beneath the rubble of his double-wide mobile home. The Tuscaloosa News reported, "He had one arm around a cinder block piling and another around his pet Labrador. The dog survived and its whining attracted rescuers after more than two hours of searching."

Another marina near the Cooks' property, Eagle Cove, took a direct hit. About a dozen boats sunk, yet there was no loss of life. However, some were injured, and those who could walked up the long hill to the Cooks' property. Rescue vehicles initially couldn't access the scene due to all the fallen trees. Later that night, a path was cleared and the injured were transported to DCH Regional Medical Center.

Ed and Shirley lived on their cruiser at Hide-A-Way Harbor after the tornado. A few weeks later, they decided their boat was just too small and they bought a larger, 38-foot boat that had two bedrooms and two bathrooms. They would live there for three months.

During that time living on the boat they made the decision to purchase another mobile home and put it on the exact same spot as the one that was destroyed. They moved

into their new home in July 2011, and were the first residents to move back into the neighborhood.
Oddly enough, the only things that remained on their lot were two big shrubs. Shirley pulled them back up with a rope, and she tells me the shrubs are alive and well today and look "real pretty". Later the Cooks also made the decision to invest in an underground tornado shelter.

Shirley tells me they survived the April 27, 2011 tornado simply because "it wasn't their time to go". Her mind drifts back to that horrible day when the wind picks up, and the sky darkens. She tells me she is horrified by tornadoes, but is comforted by their tornado shelter.

Shirley and Ed Cook

Those who lived through the tornado in Peterson got little to no attention from the media in the days, weeks, and months after the disaster. These are wonderful people who have learned to persevere. Eagle Cove Marina is being rebuilt and the community is doing very well today.

But, they will all be the first to tell you that tornadoes impact real people at a real place at a real time.

CHAPTER 19: AN ANGEL IS LOST

One of the best parts of my job is traveling to schools, doing weather programs. Most of them are elementary schools; I love older kids as well, but I connect very well with third graders. Those are "my people"... I would teach third grade science if I didn't do the weather on television. I typically visit one to two schools daily from August through May. In June and July, I do weather talks almost daily to kids in summer programs across the state. I love getting children excited about science.

One of the benefits of being on the road daily is gaining a unique knowledge of the geography of Alabama. You would be hard-pressed to think of any place in our state, within 100 miles of Birmingham, that I haven't visited in my 40-plus years of service. I have been to places you have never heard of.

There is a good chance you probably don't know about Knightens Crossroads. It is pretty much just a wide spot in the road along U.S. 278 in Northeast Alabama between Gadsden and Piedmont, near the Etowah/Calhoun county line.

At that spot, you will find a Chevron station where Ballplay Road, Roy Webb Road, and U.S. 278 come together. If you are traveling east from Gadsden, a right turn on Roy Webb Road takes you down to Jacksonville, and a left turn on Ballplay Road takes you to, as you might imagine, Ballplay. And yes, Ballplay is a real community; it was so named because Native Americans would play stickball at the site in order to resolve disputes between tribes.

In April, 2011, the Stillwell family lived in a cabin in Knightens Crossroads. On April 27, the same parent thunderstorm that produced the Tuscaloosa/Birmingham EF-4 dropped another monster in St. Clair County, producing serious damage as it moved northeast, in places like Shoal Creek Valley, Ohatchee, and Webster's Chapel. It was headed right for the Knightens Crossroads community.

The Stillwell home in April 2011, before the tornado.

Danny and Rita Stillwell, their daughter Angel (13), and son Nick (19), saw and heard the tornado coming, and they sought shelter in the crawl space under their home. As it approached, Rita told me it was like everything went into slow motion. Nick said something told him to get out; he left the crawl space and rode out the storm in a vehicle on the property that had been damaged by a fallen tree. He survived and was somehow uninjured.

When it was over, Nick heard other family members crying for help. The tornado had literally picked the cabin up, turned it, and dropped it. The cabin was mostly intact, but the way it came down resulted in Rita and Angel being trapped and pinned in the crawl space between support blocks and joists. Danny was injured but was able to get out.

Nick called 911 and went looking for help, but the first responders had a hard time getting there due to all of the fallen trees and downed power lines. Neighbors, however, were able to reach them, doing everything possible to free Rita and Angel, without much luck.

In April 2011 Josh Morgan was a deputy with the Etowah County Sheriff's Department, assigned to their investigation division. April 27 was a regular day for him, working regular cases on the 8a.m. to 4p.m. shift. He was aware of the severe weather threat, and everyone was ready to perform extra duty in the event it was needed.

Deputy Morgan was among a group of first responders that were finally able to get through to the Stillwell home that night, and he saw the situation was serious. He actually got under the damaged home, in the crawl space, to find the two people trapped. Morgan told me he is a smaller person, so he was able to get in that very small space.

Rita was close to the opening of the crawl space, but Angel was farther back. While another Deputy, Johnny Grant, was with Rita, Morgan was able to get close to Angel, and saw she was seriously injured. He did his best to talk to her and keep her calm in that desperate situation.

While Deputy Morgan was in that crawl space with Rita and Angel, the house, which was unstable, could have easily collapsed on top of all of them. But Josh told me he never thought about it until it was over. At the point when Sheriff Todd Entrekin, who arrived on the scene, encouraged Morgan and Grant to get out of the crawl space due to the danger of a collapse, and the rumor of another storm approaching. But, they refused to leave Rita and Angel.

Rita told me she clearly remembers the deputies told her they were not going to leave them until they were out of the crawl space. She said, "I want to give those guys credit, because I don't think anyone else would have stayed with us knowing the house could have fallen at any time."

Angel, despite being seriously injured and most likely in shock, was alert and talking to Deputy Morgan. She could tell him who she was, her age, and the name of her school. They were having a calm conversation, with Morgan telling Angel they were working hard to get her out. This continued for at least an hour, but it was clear that Angel's condition was deteriorating.

Deputy Morgan could see one of the floor joists was sitting on Angel, and some of the big blocks that were used to hold the floor joists up were on her back.

Outside, a big group of volunteer firefighters and neighbors were trying to use jacks to lift up the house, so Rita and Angel could be pulled out. Rescue-type hammers were also brought in, and given to the deputies, who chipped away at the blocks in the crawl space. Rita was freed first, then later Angel was pulled out.

Both Rita and Angel were taken to Gadsden Regional Medical Center. Rita had a broken pelvis, six broken vertebrae, nine broken ribs. and punctured lungs. She was in the hospital for one month and then spent time in a rehabilitation facility. Rita is doing fine today and lives in Florida.

Angel was pronounced dead after midnight that night. Rita was taken to see Angel briefly to say goodbye in the hospital.

Deb Stillwell, a family friend, firefighter, and EMT at Ballplay #1 Volunteer Fire Department, was one of the first on the scene on April 27, 2011. She remembers Angel as a different kind of 13-year-old who looked like she was grown. She was a sixth-grader at Pleasant Valley School, and had just started playing softball that year.

**Memorial marker for Angel Stillwell
at Pleasant Valley School**

Rita says Angel had a very big heart and would protect anybody. She wanted to be a veterinarian when she finished school because she loved animals.

Angel Stillwell, photo taken April 24, 2011

For their work that night, Deputies Josh Morgan, Johnny Grant, and Reserve Deputy Michael Bishop earned the Medal of Valor from the Etowah County Sheriff's Department. These were three of the many heroes of April 27, 2011, in Alabama.

CHAPTER 20: THERE ARE GOOD PEOPLE IN THE WORLD

On April 27, 2011, University of Alabama student Paige Rawls was awakened by a call from her mother at 5:00 a.m. telling her to keep an eye out because there were tornados headed her way. She lived off of 15th Street, right behind Schlotzkey's Deli in Tuscaloosa. She was so aggravated with her mom because she didn't have class that day and had planned on sleeping in. After the call, she went upstairs to wake her roommates so they could make sure to pay attention to the weather.

That storm passed through without any damage at their place, but it left them without power. After going back to sleep, Paige got up and worked on term papers with her laptop running on battery power. Her mom continued to call throughout the day, reminding Paige to watch the weather because it was supposed to be bad. Paige was scheduled to go to work at Target, but she called in because she had to finish her papers.

Earlier that month, on April 15, she was at work when a tornado moved through the southern and eastern part of Tuscaloosa. Paige came home to her roommates having a tornado party upstairs. On that day there was no damage around 15th Street and no worries.

April 27, according to Paige, was different somehow. Her mother kept calling. Her uncles called. Everyone wanted to make sure she was in a safe place. She actually decided to be a smart aleck and put pillows and blankets in the pantry under the stairs because as she told me, "If my family is going to drive me crazy, I'm going to be comfortable". Paige wouldn't say she was ever concerned. She did wake her roommates up and made them come downstairs, "just in case".

That afternoon, Paige and her roommates turned live severe weather coverage on ABC 33/40 and watched the tornado move into Tuscaloosa. She then thought, "Holy cow! That's us!" They all ran to the pantry, where they had the pillows and blankets. Paige had to coerce her dog because he didn't want to get in the pantry with them.

As soon as they closed the door, it was there. They held the pillows over their heads and Paige repeated, "We're ok! We're ok! We're gonna be okay!" over and over. One of her roommates was praying, one was crying, the other silent. Paige heard glass breaking and things hitting the walls. This seemed like it went on for at least five minutes. It was only seconds in reality. Then it was silent.

Her roommate tried to open the door but it was jammed. After some work, they finally got out and saw their second story was gone. The back door was open, and all the windows were broken. They climbed out of the front door and it looked like a war zone that had just been bombed. People were yelling for help in all directions. Paige got one call out to her mom, who was in the storm cellar in Brilliant, in Marion County. "Umm, the house is gone but we're okay". She thought Paige was joking at first. Paige said it again and then they got disconnected. Paige's mom later told her that when she said it the second time, she heard the terror in her voice.

**The home where Paige Rawls and her
roommates survived an EF-4 tornado
just off 15th Street in Tuscaloosa.
Photo from Darla Rawls.**

Paige tried to help people where she could. Her
roommates made bandages out of their clothing. They
walked to 15th Street; seeing some of the people was like
watching a horror movie. There were people with cuts,
ears bleeding, skin just hanging.

Then, in this chaos, they were told another tornado was
headed their way. Their house was severely damaged,
and it couldn't withstand another tornado. So they
headed toward University Mall as a potential shelter but
were unable to get inside.

As they were standing outside, trying to figure out what to do (cell service was out), a truck of guys pulled up and told them another tornado was on the way and they needed to get somewhere. They decided to try Home Depot. The boys in the truck drove them there.

Home Depot on that day was their saving grace. They let them in, took them to their breakroom, offered them their food, and just let them be there. Paige kept having crying spells and her dog wouldn't sit down. The Home Depot employees took her dog outside and kept him preoccupied while another employee tried to comfort her. The employees stayed there until 11:30 p.m. with Paige and her roommates until her dad and uncle got there

Paige Rawl's Nissan was under this debris pile after the tornado. Photo from Darla Rawls.

Paige tells me she didn't hear any of the employees at Home Depot complain, but instead, they offered her support and comfort and the lunches they had brought. Paige says she will never forget the employees in the Home Depot in Tuscaloosa for the compassion they showed her that night.

Paige remembers the days following the tornado when she came back to salvage what she could. Seeing the unity of the community was one of the most amazing things to her. Strangers helping strangers, passing out water, food, or just offering a hug. It was the realization that there are good people in the world; you just have to open your eyes.

Paige Rawls is now Paige Ketchum; she lives with her husband and children in Mississippi. She tells me she still has anxiety, and sometimes panic attacks during severe weather situations. And to this day she can't watch any TV specials or reports on the April 27, 2011 tornado outbreak. She is simply thankful that because of the grace of God she lived through a horrifying violent tornado on a spring day in Tuscaloosa, Alabama.

Paige Ketchum, her husband (Adam), her stepson (Hayden), and their twins (Maddux and McKenna). Photo from Paige Ketchum.

CHAPTER 21: IMAGES

I have gathered literally thousands of images from April 27, 2011, and the days afterward. I have selected a few for this book to reflect the widespread nature of the damage and suffering across our state. These are not the highest quality pictures; the iPhone didn't come along until 2007, and some of these images were captured by flip phones.

Also, they are generally not from larger cities. Most of them were taken in places you probably have never heard of in rural parts of Alabama. You hear it over and over... pictures and video, even the graphic ones, don't really convey the horror of a tornado outbreak. But I think this collection will give you some idea of what people experienced on that horrible Wednesday in late April 2011. Not just in Tuscaloosa and Birmingham, but statewide.

A rain wrapped, violent EF-4 tornado crossing U.S. 431 in northern Calhoun County, near the Colwell/Webster's Chapel communities. Photo from Brandon Harris.

A man, forlorn and exhausted, sitting in the midst
of all that he had, reduced to a pile of rubble in
Hackleburg. This tornado was rated EF-5.
Photo from Kalai Kennedy-Lynam.

**Precious Necale Fegans-Hartley, who was killed
in the Shadydale Trailer Park just east of Pell City.
She shielded her small children as trees came
down on them due to straight-line winds;
both of them survived.
Photo from Angela Garrett.**

**The Wrangler Distribution Center in
Hackleburg, destroyed by an EF-5 tornado.
Photo from Brandy Pugh.**

Damage in the Aldridge community of Walker County from an EF-4 tornado. This tornado would go on to hit Cordova minutes later.
Photo from Jeff Carr.

Mountain View Baptist Church in Phil Campbell, destroyed by an EF-5 tornado that passed nearby. Photo from Bart Moss.

This trailer home in Hale County, northeast of Greensboro, was destroyed by an EF-3 tornado April 27, 2011. One person was home; she was injured, but survived. Photo from Shandy Andrews.

Freida Thomason, in front of her destroyed home in Concord, west of Birmingham. She had a brain bleed, broken hand, and was bruised from head to toe, but she survived the EF-4 tornado. Photo from Dale Atkins.

Arguably the most violent tornado of the outbreak, this is the EF-5 in Marion County near Hackleburg. It was on the ground for 132 miles, killing 72 people, before dissipating in southern Tennessee.
Photo from Ronald Elrod.

Eddie and Teresa Hall lost their life in their home in Hackleburg on April 27, 2011. Photo from their daughter, April Price.

This home was destroyed by an EF-4 tornado in the
small community of Boley Springs, in Fayette
County. Two people survived here.
Photo from Jennifer Dove.

Home destroyed by an EF-5 in the Chalybeate Springs community of Lawrence County. Twelve people, all in the same family, survived here in a tornado shelter. Photo from Amy Stewart.

04/28/2011

This home was destroyed by an EF-4 tornado in southern Cherokee County at Goshen; two people survived in the structure. This was less than two miles away from the Goshen United Methodist Church, whose building was destroyed by another EF-4 tornado on Palm Sunday, March 27, 1994. Photo from Janet Woods.

**Damage from the EF-5 tornado at
Hackleburg, in Marion County.
Photo from Darren O'Neal.**

The Eoline Volunteer Fire Department, in Bibb County, destroyed by an EF-3 tornado. Twelve people from the community sought shelter here; they survived in the small room still standing. Photo from Sharon Chambers.

This home and a 65-acre farm in the High Point
community of DeKalb County was wiped out
April 27, 2011. The Warren family lost all of their
barns, buildings, and their home. They were in
the home when it was destroyed, but they survived.
Four neighbors were killed.
Photo from Melissa Warren.

Damage from an EF-4 tornado in the Pratt City
community in Birmingham.
Photo from Brandy Culpepper.

EF-4 tornado in northern Blount County, near Blountsville. Same one that hit Cordova earlier in the evening. Photo from Polly Morris.

Steve Hayes (center) sitting on the foundation of his home destroyed by an EF-4 tornado at Union Grove in Marshall County. Alongside Hayes are Craig Williams and Talley Hayes (Steve's brother). Photo from Karen Hayes.

The EF-4 tornado moving through Fultondale as seen from the 16th floor of the City Federal Building in downtown Birmingham.
Photo from Katie Ross.

Pat and Kim Renfroe lost their home near
East Limestone High School. This was the
same tornado that destroyed much of
Hackleburg and Phil Campbell.
Photo from DeAnna Haataja.

This cabin was destroyed by an EF-4 tornado at Lake Martin. The residents left before the tornado moved through; a life-saving decision.
Photo from Allen Cox.

Some of the damage in Cullman; the downtown area was hit by an EF-4 tornado. Photo from Julie Knop.

CHAPTER 22: THE IMAGE

Jeff Roberts was born March 6, 1961. He grew up in western Jefferson County in the Concord community, and attended Concord Elementary School. He developed an interest in photography; well-known photojournalist Spider Martin was one of his mentors. Roberts would join the Birmingham News staff as a part-timer in May 1993.

Jeff's colleague, John Archibald, a columnist for AL.com and the Birmingham News, tells me that he was a great story teller, and a hard worker. He had a big heart and was a "humble sort of guy".

Jeff Roberts

On April 27, 2011, Roberts was positioned in the western part of the Birmingham metro, and somehow was caught in the path of the approaching supercell thunderstorm that contained a violent, EF-4 tornado. This was the same one that tore up Tuscaloosa, and was nearing his location in Concord. John Archibald tells me that John drove his car to a gas station, and parked by a row of gas pumps, the worst possible place to be during a tornado. As it turned out the tornado missed Jeff's location by only about 100 yards. After the storm passed, he simply couldn't get far because of debris and downed trees and power lines.

Even though he grew up in Concord, Roberts was disoriented. He could hear people crying for help, and destruction was everywhere. Jeff started to feel dizzy, as though he was having a heart attack. He wanted so badly to help all those people, but didn't know what to do. He caught his breath, and called 911 asking for help. He went down a street, checking on people and reassuring them that help was on the way. After realizing he did everything he could do, it was time to grab the camera.

Two of those he checked on were Faye and Willie Hyde, who just lost their home in the tornado in Concord. Shortly after 6:00 p.m., Jeff saw Faye Hyde hugging and comforting her granddaughter, two-year-old Sierra Goldsmith. They were sitting on a mattress in the front yard of their destroyed home.

He then took a photo of that scene, and it was the "shot seen around the world". Jeff's photo of Mrs. Hyde and Sierra was on the front page of the Birmingham News the next day, and was ultimately seen in newspapers globally.

Faye Hyde and Sierra Goldsmith on April 27, 2011. Photo by Jeff Roberts, permission granted by AL.com/Alabama Media Group.

Front page of the Birmingham News, April 28, 2011

The next year Jeff would be part of a group laid off in the newspaper's transition to digital. He became ill shortly after learning the news, and died in November 2012. But many still today are thankful for this one photo that perhaps defined his career, and told the story of a tornado tragedy in the Deep South. One picture is indeed worth a thousand words.

CHAPTER 23: LESSONS LEARNED

In the days and months following April 27, 2011, I had nothing to say in person about the day. I needed to grieve. In fact, I went through every emotion during the grief process. Denial, anger, guilt, depression, and acceptance. It took about six months to work through it all.

I can recall going through the damage in Tuscaloosa County with a group of government officials on Saturday, April 30. We toured Holt and Alberta City, and I actually broke away before the group got to 15th Street in Tuscaloosa. I had simply seen enough. For five years through high school and college, I worked at WTBC radio, located on 15th Street across from Forest Lake. It was my world for so long as a teenager, and I just didn't have the guts to see it. It would be June before I finally drove through that part of town. It still took my breath away.

It just so happened the National Weather Association annual meeting was in Birmingham in the fall of 2011, and I still had nothing to say. Many were very surprised, but it just wasn't the time for me to speak. I was on the steering committee, and at the conference every day during the week-long event, but I did not speak. Very odd for the loud mouth guy from Birmingham that always has something to say.

As most do, I pretty much kept my mental struggles to myself during those six months. After all, I have been doing this for decades. I have worked countless tornado events in my career, and went through the 1974

Superoutbreak as a student volunteer. After April 27 I should have been confident, bold, outspoken, and a leader. But internally I felt weak, guilty, and defeated.

And it is not just me. Teams from the National Weather Service conducted storm surveys while search and rescue or recovery operations were ongoing in the days after April 27. Many of these meteorologists were ill-prepared for interacting with survivors and the impact on themselves. Counseling services from the NOAA Employee Assistance Program were used at NWS offices in Birmingham and Huntsville to help their employees cope with their experience.

For too long nobody wanted to talk about mental health. The truth is that it impacts EVERY family if you peel back a layer or two. I am so thankful for Ginger Zee, my former intern and chief meteorologist for ABC News, for speaking out about her struggle with depression. Ten days before she started her job at ABC, she checked herself into a mental health hospital. Her book "Natural Disaster: I Cover Them. I am One", is a must read for professional meteorologists, and for anyone with mental health struggles.

I almost feel guilty opening up about the issues we face as meteorologists. After all, we are not in combat, we are not first responders, and we don't rush toward a burning building to save people. Many of us in television like me basically are in front of a green wall in a safe, dry studio when the weather turns violent.

But we do face depression, anxiety, and impostor syndrome, a psychological pattern in which an individual doubts their skills, talents or accomplishments and has a persistent internalized fear of being exposed as a "fraud". Feelings of self-doubt and failure are very real to us, along with the perception that we are being negatively evaluated and judged.

You miss forecasts, Sometimes, high impact forecasts like "Snowmageddon" in 2014. People are injured, and some die during tornado events you work. It really goes beyond a football coach losing a game or two. You will never understand it unless you walk a mile in our shoes.

Social media has amplified the issue. When I started doing weather on television in 1978, people would have to send a letter, or make a phone call to express hateful feedback. But now, everyone has a phone, and platforms like Facebook and Twitter have become a place of bile, hate, vitriol, and weapons-grade ignorance. It has become very easy to become a widely seen hater.

Let me stress here, we need critical feedback. We will never get better unless we listen carefully to those who use our products and services. Not every negative comment is from a "troll, hater, or know-it-all". Some are important and give us an opportunity to improve. But much of what we see is meant to inflict as much pain as possible on us.

My standard line is that "you can't hurt my feelings; I don't have any feelings left to hurt". To some degree that is true, but even crusty old weather people like me can still be vulnerable. The bottom line is that being a meteorologist is simply not good for your mental health. But you learn to persevere if you do this long enough.

As the calendar rolled over to 2012, I knew it was time to get to work. I wanted to know why so many died, and what we needed to do to fix it.

I believe the biggest lesson learned was that what we do is not enough. My background is engineering and physical science. I know very little about communicating risk and human behavior. Yes, I do hang out at Dollar General and Walmart stores talking to people, but that isn't enough.

Many social science professionals reached out to me, knowing the pain and needs in the professional meteorological community after April 27, 2011. Their offer to help was immediately welcomed. Physical science must be integrated with social science to make the severe weather warning process work effectively. Over the past ten years I have become close friends with many in social science; their data and research has proven to be invaluable. An interdisciplinary approach is the only way to move forward.

After working with social scientists, reading countless papers on the mortality of April 27, and talking with people we serve across all of the various demographic groups, I believe I have some firm conclusions on what happened. Why in the world did over 250 people die when the warnings for all 62 tornadoes were so good?

1. THE SIREN MENTALITY. Despite it being technology that mostly originated in World War Two, most people in the U.S. today still honestly believe they are going to hear an outdoor warning siren before the arrival of a tornado. This mentality has killed countless numbers of Americans over the years.

The truth is you won't be able to hear an outdoor siren in a home, business, school, or church during a raging storm or in the middle of the night. Sure, you can probably hear them on a sunny day at 3 in the afternoon, but what good does that do? Sirens have NEVER been effective at reaching people indoors. Never. The only purpose they serve is reaching a limited number of people outdoors. That's it. If a siren is your main method of knowing a tornado is approaching your home, then you pretty much have no hope. We have to move past them. There are days I want to climb up on those poles, take the sirens down, and burn them. That way you know you won't hear them.

Some municipalities and county governments are in the process of decommissioning outdoor sirens. They are so costly to maintain, and do little good. If we don't move past the siren mentality, then more and more people will die during tornado events.

Everyone needs two ways of hearing a tornado warning, and a siren is NOT one of them. The baseline is a NOAA Weather Radio, with your smartphone being the secondary way.

NOAA Weather Radio does not work on a cellular network; it is an independent RF network that is very reliable. Every home in a tornado prone area must have one. And, on your smartphone, be sure WEA (Wireless Emergency Alerts) are enabled. This has nothing to do with an app; every phone in the U.S. comes with this service. And, beyond WEA, have a good app designed for weather warnings on your phone as well.

2. LACK OF HELMET USE. Very few people, especially adults, take the time to wear protective headgear when they are in a tornado warning polygon. I really stepped up stressing the importance of this in recent years. By putting on a bicycle helmet, a batting helmet, or a motorcycle helmet, you greatly enhance your chance of surviving a tornado. Most of the serious injuries during a tornado involve blunt force trauma to the skull region.

   In 2012, scientists at the UAB Injury Control Research Center (ICRC) published a research-driven commentary suggesting that helmets are an essential addition to an individual's tornado-safety preparations.

   In the commentary, the researchers recommend "the use of any helmet, or head covering made of a hard material and worn to protect the head from injury, stored in an easily and readily accessible location in the home, workplace or vehicle for which one of its purposes is to be worn in the event of or threat of tornadic activity."

They describe a safety helmet as any structurally sound helmet, such as a motorcycle helmet, football helmet, baseball helmet, bicycle helmet, skateboard helmet, or even a construction hardhat; as long as the helmet's original intended purpose is to minimize anatomical damage sustained as a result of high-velocity impacts.

Everybody in the family needs to wear a helmet during a tornado warning, including adults. I should also mention here everyone needs hard sole shoes (in case you have to walk over a tornado debris field), and a portable air horn (so first responders can find you if you are injured and can't move, or verbally communicate with them).

3. TOO MANY FALSE ALARMS. This one is on us. In 2011, the FAR (False Alarm Radio) in Birmingham was hovering around 80. Meaning, 8 out of 10 tornado warnings were false alarms. I have heard this over and over… "I hear tornado warnings often, and nothing ever happens". It is the classic "cry wolf" syndrome. After a while, people hear a tornado warning and do absolutely nothing because of the high FAR.

Thankfully, meteorologists at the National Weather Service in Birmingham, led by Science Operations Officer Kevin Laws, went back to basic science to solve the problem in the years following April 27, 2011. The FAR has dropped from 80 to around 35 today, a figure I didn't expect to see in my lifetime.

Unfortunately the FAR is still very high in other parts of the country; I am hoping all NWS offices will consider the issue and work toward lower values (while keeping the Probability of Detection high). The easiest thing to do is issue a warning if you see rotation on radar, or get a report of a wall cloud or funnel cloud. But, often, the right thing to do is to keep your finger off the trigger. Yes, you will miss one from time to time, but constant bogus warnings will do lots of harm to the process.

And, part of the issue is simply not understanding how warnings are issued. On October 1st, 2007, the National Weather Service introduced storm-based warnings for tornadoes, severe thunderstorms, flash floods, and marine hazards that are more geographically specific for these short-duration events. When issuing a warning, the National Weather Service uses geometric shapes (polygons), as opposed to issuing a warning for the entire county.

Sometimes, only a very small part of a county is placed under a warning. But, when people hear their county mentioned, they believe the entire county should be taking action. Storm based warnings are excellent since tornadoes are small and counties are big. But we have to teach people how the storm-based/polygon system works. This is where the James Spann line "respect the polygon" came from.

4. POOR COMMUNICATION WITH CERTAIN PEOPLE GROUPS: I did a poor job of reaching certain groups of people, like Hispanics. During a tornado, it is my job to reach everyone and mitigate loss of life. It doesn't matter if you are right wing or left wing, young or old, black or white, or speak English or Spanish. I didn't lift a finger to help Hispanics in our audience. They couldn't understand what I was saying, and couldn't make much sense out of the radar or tornado locations. We have to do better in the future.

5. GEOGRAPHY ILLITERACY: Most people can't find their house on a map. And, we mostly use maps during long form tornado coverage. With today's smartphones and the turn-by-turn directions, you really don't need good map skills. But everyone should be able to put a dot on a blank map with state and county lines within 50 miles of your house. Knowing your county, and the adjacent counties, is absolutely crucial.

The lack of geographical knowledge is why you often hear me call out barbeque joints, Walmarts, barns, and wide spots in the road. People know and understand those locations that are near where they live. But as meteorologists we must be more proactive in getting people to learn a little geography before big severe weather days.

6. WAITING UNTIL VISUAL CONFIRMATION: I guess it is just human nature, but studies have shown that many people don't go to their safe place until they actually see a tornado, in person or on television. This is from the April 27, 2011 Service Assessment published by the National Weather Service:

"Visual confirmation of a threat is often the most significant motivator for protective action. As previously mentioned, many respondents needed visual confirmation of the tornado before seeking shelter. While warnings often put people on alert and motivated them to obtain more information, it was seeing the tornado or its effects that provided the impetus to seek shelter. It is important to note that visual confirmation of large tornadoes was particularly difficult in this event. Most people do not know what a large tornado looks like (i.e., a large, dark, low-hanging cloud) and were not expecting what they actually saw. People reported that they spent several minutes looking directly at the tornado before they realized what it was. In many cases, it was not until people saw debris flying that they recognized the threat. This fact, coupled with the speed of the storms, meant many people barely made it to shelters or did not make it to safety."

The bottom line for us is that we have to do a better job of getting tornadoes on camera so they can be shown on live television. On April 27, 2011, tornadoes were on the ABC 33/40

SKYCAM network before they tore into Cullman and Tuscaloosa, and some were captured by spotter dashcams. But, most of them had no visual presentation other than radar.

Even if we see an intense "hook echo" and velocity couplet, and strongly word the dangerous nature of the storm, many do nothing because they don't actually see the tornado. Radar to them is nothing more than a bucket of spilled paint.

The problem we have here in the Deep South is that most of our tornadoes are rain-wrapped, and many of them happen at night. It is simply impossible to show them live, and for people to see them as they approach. We must communicate this message strongly.

The bottom line here is that we ALL have work to do. The weather enterprise, those in emergency management, and the public.

In the years following the 2011 outbreak, before every severe weather threat, I would see the question "Will this be like April 27???" I really don't like the question, and generally speaking, won't answer it.

Days like April 27, 2011, are generational. They tend to happen about every 40 years in Alabama. You can see the pattern: March 21, 1932… April 3, 1974… April 27, 2011. So no, there is an extremely high probability that the event in question won't produce as many tornadoes as one of these days.

But understand this. If there is only one tornado in the entire state, and if that tornado comes right down your street, then that day is YOUR April 27. We have to be ready for every severe weather event, not just the ones that are historic in nature.

CHAPTER 24: 252 SOULS

Their earthly journey ended as a direct result of the April 27, 2011 tornado outbreak in Alabama. We won't forget you.

Candice Hope Abernathy, 23
Kammie Abernathy, 5
Rodney Gene Ables, 51
Minnie Acklin, 73
Matthew Chase Adams, 21
Ovella P. Andrews, 81
Jeffrey Artis, 51
Oberia Layton Ashley, 86
Scott Atterton, 23
Milton Edward Baker Sr., 68
Jennifer V. Bayode, 35
Donna Renee Berry, 52
Chelsie Black, 20
Nila Black, 68
Zan Reese Black, 45
Caiden Blair, 2 months
Charlotte Bludsworth, 36
Belinda Boatner, 67
Eddie Joe Bobbitt, 71
Michael Bowers, 3
Gregory John Braden, 58
Samuel Brasfield, 50
Bessie Brewster, 72
Bridget Barnwell Brisbois, 34
Cora L. Brown, 68
Gerald C. Brown, 70
Kathleen Brown, 64
Loryn Brown, 21

Michelle Brown, 43
Mary Bryant, 43
Gene Bullock, 65
Marcella Bullock, 64
Iva Mae Cantrell, 73
James Jerry Clements, 66
Cheryl Denise Cooper, 47
Katie Cornwell, 15
Jeffrey Dewight Cotham, 35
Jack Cox, 78
Robbie Cox, 68
Charlene Crochet, 41
Earl Lewis Crosby Sr., 63
Hugh Graham Davie, 55
Ta' Christianna Dixon, 11 months
Tina Donais, 37
Jonathan Doss, 12
Justin Doss, 10
Ruby Douthitt, 61
Danielle Downs, 24
Chris Dunn, 32
Mike Daworld Dunn, 58
Canatha Hyde Earley, 71
Arielle Edwards, 22
Makayla Edwards, 5
Jewell Ewing, 73
Melgium Farley, 58
Precious Necale Fegans-Hartley, 27
Emma Ferguson, 6
Jeremy Ferguson, 34
Tawnya Ferguson, 32
Harold Fitzgerald, 65
Michael Forrest, 54
Tina Forrest, 49

Carol Lisa Fox, 50
Melissa Ann "Missy" Myers Gantt, 43
Charles Tommy Garner, 75
Mae Garner, 79
Donnie Gentry, 63
Patricia Ann Gentry, 50
Hannah Goins, 3
Kenneth Graham, 56
Linda Graham, 61
Aurelia Guzman, 12
Ruth Hairston, 90
Zora Lee Jones Hale, 80
Milinia Nicole "Nikki" Hammonds, 32
Eddie Hall, 53
Janet Dickinson Hall, 55
Teresa Gay Hall, 50
Ann Hallmark, 54
Jayden Hallmark, 17 months
Jennifer Hallmark, 31
Phillip Hallmark, 56
Shane Hallmark, 37
Kathy Gray Haney, 46
Calvin Hannah, 81
Harold Harcrow, 74
Patricia Harcrow, 75
Cedria Harris, 8
Keshun Harris, 5
Lloyd Winford Harris, 68
Ashley Harrison, 22
Donald Ray Heaps, 48
Robert Gene Hicks, 83
Jerry Lee Hodge, 64
Lester William Hood, 81
Jody Huizenga, 28

Shena Hutchins, 26
Leah Isbell, 7
Ronnie Isbell, 56
Tammy Isbell, 31
Lethel Izell, 86
Carolyn Ann Jackson, 50
Jacqueline Jefferson, 45
Harold "Junior" Jett, 47
Pam Jett, 43
Tammy Johnson, 52
Donna Lee "Leah" Jokela, 77
Kaarlo Jokela, 76
Francis Arvella Jones, 72
Garrett Jones, 25
Jennifer Leonard Jones, 26
Leota Jones, 97
Reba Jones, 75
Bertha S. Kage, 91
James Robert Keller Jr., 67
Helen Kemp, 80
Jeffery Kemp, 60
Reba Kemp, 60
Jimmy Michael Kilgore, 48
Linda Faye Knight, 57
Rickey Ethan Knox, 10
Thelma Krallman, 89
Haley Alexis Kreider, 8
Michael David Kreider, 10
Michelle Pearson Kreider, 30
Davis Lynn Latham, 57
Tennie Mozelle Lancaster, 95
Amy LeClere, 33
Jay W. LeClere, 45
Alice Herren Lee, 74

Lee Andrew Lee, 88
Thomas Carl Lee, 64
Velma T. Leroy, 64
Dorothy Lewis, 61
Henry Lewis, 26
Thomas D. Lewis, 66
Dagmar Leyden, 56
Linda Sue Lipscomb, 63
William Lipscomb, 67
Freddie Lollie, 81
Vickey Lollie, 55
Stella "Mae" Lovell, 97
Carrie Grier Lowe, 26
Frankie Lunsford, 55
John Lynch, 70
Katherine Massa, 70
Lyndon Lee "Doby" Mayes, 74
Mary Mayes, 76
Yvonne Mayes, 61
Cledis Inez McCarley, 69
Sandra Gayle McCrory, 56
Carol Jan McElyea, 67
Courtney McGaha, 15
Ronnie McGaha, 40
Vicki Lynn McKee, 47
Christian A. McNeil, 15 months
William Robert McPherson, 85
Zy'Queria McShan, 2
Martha Michaels, 72
William Michaels, 70
Eula Miller, 80
Melanie Nicole Mixon, 26
Claudia I. Mojica, 38
Edgar Mojica, 9

Bobby Joe Moore, 61
Kelli Thorn Morgan, 24
Michael Morgan, 32
Vernon Spencer Motes, 33
Ernest C. "Ernie" Mundi Jr., 53
Philomena Muotoe, 79
Martha Ann Gray Myers, 67
Kenneth Ray Nation, 64
Edna Lucille Bradley Nix, 89
Faye O'Kelley, 70
Ida Ott, 87
Timothy Ott, 53
Martha Lou Pace, 64
J.W. Parker, 78
Perry Blake Peek, 24
Lola Pitts, 85
Sandra Pledger, 68
Terrilyn Plump, 37
Frederick Post, 72
Deniece Presley, 57
Donald "Duck" Ray, 73
Jacob Ralph Ray, 5
Virginia Revis, 53
Colvin Rice, 78
Kevin Rice, 36
Janice Dorothy Peden Riddle, 54
Roger Glen Riddle, 55
James Romaine, 65
Ester Rosson, 81
Shannon Gail Sampson, 39
Albert Sanders, 44
Angie Sanders, 43
Ramona Sanders-Walker, 47
Ann Satterfield, 81

Herbert Satterfield, 90
Annie Lois Humphries Sayer, 88
Georgia Schribner, 83
Janie Shannon, 80
Shelby Jean Shannon, 58
Judy Sherrill, 62
Morgan Marlene Sigler, 23
Annette Singleton, 45
Helen Smith, 84
Horace Grady Smith, 83
Marcus Smith, 21
Ricky Paul Smith, 55
Peggy Sparks, 55
Leon Spruell, 76
Sylvia Spruell, 69
Wesley Starr, 45
William Chance Stevens, 22
Angel Stillwell, 13
Keenan Jonathan Sullivan, 20
Rachel Renee Tabor, 37
Jack E. Tenhaeff, 67
Allen O'Neal Terry, 49
Herman O'Neal Terry, 80
Justin Le'Eric Thomas, 15
Louella Bell Thompson, 81
Terry Tinker, 50
Sonya Black Trapp, 47
Tracy A. Traweek, 39
Patricia Turner, 55
Willie Lee Turner III, 21
Jackson Van Horn, 24
Ken Vaughn, 24
Daniel Vermillion, 42
Jidal Vermillion, 44

Edward Vuknic, 66
Carroll Dean "C.D." Waller, 76
Gerri Waller, 64
Branen Warren, 13
Lucille Waters, 89
Elizabeth C. White, 25
Judith White, 63
Wayne White, 68
Elease Whited, 75
John Whited, 77
Alan Mark Wideman, 49
Jeanette Cochran Wideman, 52
Nancy L. Wilson, 56
Charlie Andrew Wolfe, 68
Nettie Ruth Wolfe, 68
Rebecca Herren Woodall, 70
Herbert Wooten, 70
Juanita Wooten, 70
Helen Wurm, 98

There was one more death in addition to the 251 listed here; a baby of six months gestation. The mother was seriously injured and went into premature labor after her home on Ray Wyatt Road in St. Clair County was destroyed.

She was taken to UAB Hospital; the baby was delivered April 30, 2011 and died May 3, 2011.